As one of the world's longest establishe[d]
and best-known travel brand[s]
Thomas Cook are the experts in trave[l]

For more than 135 years ou[r]
guidebooks have unlocked the secrets
of destinations around the world,
sharing with travellers a wealth of
experience and a passion for travel.

**Rely on Thomas Cook as your
travelling companion on your next trip
and benefit from our unique heritage.**

Thomas Cook **traveller** guides

KERALA
& SOUTHERN INDIA
Anil Mulchandani

Written by Anil Mulchandani, updated by Debbie Stowe
Original photography by CPA Media and Vasile Szakacs

Published by Thomas Cook Publishing
A division of Thomas Cook Tour Operations Limited.
Company Registration no. 3772199 England
The Thomas Cook Business Park, Unit 9, Coningsby Road,
Peterborough PE3 8SB, United Kingdom
Email: books@thomascook.com, Tel: + 44 (0) 1733 416477
www.thomascookpublishing.com

Produced by Cambridge Publishing Management Limited
Burr Elm Court, Main Street, Caldecote CB23 7NU
www.cambridgepm.co.uk

ISBN: 978-1-84848-243-2

© 2006, 2008 Thomas Cook Publishing
This third edition © 2010
Text © Thomas Cook Publishing
Maps © Thomas Cook Publishing/PCGraphics (UK) Limited

Series Editor: Linda Bass
Production/DTP: Steven Collins

Printed and bound in Italy by Printer Trento

Cover photography © Felix Hug/Getty Images

Contents

Introduction

Kerala runs along the Arabian Sea coastline of southwestern India, rising eastward from the sea to the forested peaks of the Western Ghats. The land between the sea and the mountains is fertile and produces the spices that attracted Chinese, Arab, Jewish and European traders to the harbours of Kozhikode and Kochi. Justly famous for its beaches and lush green backwaters, Kerala is among the most popular destinations in India.

Isolated for centuries from the rest of India by its natural boundaries of hills and the sea, Kerala has cities and towns with colourful temples, European-style churches, and mosques that mirror the distinctive local cultures and international influences from centuries of global maritime contact. The traders, settlers and invaders brought with them their religions, and so a healthy Christian and Muslim population balances the Hindu majority of Kerala.

While agriculture remains the mainstay of the economy, the state government and local enterprise have recognised the importance of tourism as a revenue earner and have developed a sophisticated infrastructure that presents the scenic and cultural charms of Kerala with the comfort of luxurious hotels and resorts, houseboats, restored heritage houses and plantation bungalows.

The neighbouring state of Tamil Nadu, like Kerala, has an attractive coastline with beaches, palm groves and paddy fields, and green hills rich in wildlife and spice plantations, but its appeal lies in its remarkable devotional architecture from the shore temples of Mahabalipuram and Rameshvaram to the bustling temple towns of Kanchipuram, Thanjavur and Madurai. In contrast, the former French enclave of Pondicherry has a distinctly European feel, with its churches, colonial buildings, and restaurants serving French food and wine.

Karnataka ranges scenically from some of the wettest sections of the Western Ghats near its west coast, draped in dense deciduous forests known for their wildlife, coffee estates, waterfalls and the source of great rivers like the Krishna, Kaveri and Tungabhadra, to the historic towns of the interior, surrounded by ancient granite and barren rocks. A succession of dynasties has used the rocks of Karnataka to create some of India's finest architectural gems, such as the superbly carved temples of Halebid, Belur, Hampi, Badami and Pattadakal, the majestic mosques of Bijapur and Bidar, and the grand palaces of Mysore, which was once the seat of power of the princely state that comprised much of today's Karnataka before India's independence in 1947. The capital of Karnataka today is Bangalore, the modern face of Southern India and one of the world's largest centres of information technology and software development. Bangalore is also known for its fashion garment exports.

Like Bangalore, Hyderabad, which is the capital of Andhra Pradesh, has evolved into an IT and outsourcing hub.

Once the capital of India's largest princely state, Hyderabad has impressive palaces and museums, and forts that protected the state from invasions. A few hours' drive east from Hyderabad is Nagarjunakonda, the most substantial remains of Buddhist civilisation in Southern India. The heartland of Telugu arts, crafts and culture lies further east in the fertile Krishna and Godavari deltas, whose attractions include a number of ancient sites and a living tradition of weaving which has been nurtured by the cotton production of the region.

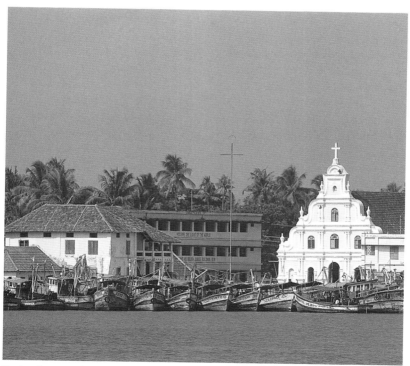

The bustling port of Kochi is the scene of much trade and business

The land

Southern India entices travellers with a variety of beautiful scenery, from fine beaches along the Arabian Sea and Bay of Bengal to hill stations like Kodaikanal, Ooty and Munnar near Anamudi Peak, which at 2,695m (8,842ft) is the highest mountain in Southern India. According to local legend, Kerala was created by Parashurama, an incarnation of Lord Vishnu, whom the gods promised as much land as he could reclaim with the hurl of an axe.

Geography

This creation myth may have its origins in geographical reality, for the coastal areas of Kerala were raised from the sea by geological forces, and the landscape has continued to evolve ever since with silt deposited by the rivers and tides. The backwaters (*see pp40–41*) are a distinctive feature of Kerala's coastal geography.

Running parallel to the coast towards the southern tip of the peninsula, the Western Ghats are richly vegetated with evergreen and deciduous forests, including some of India's most substantial tracts of rainforest and important wildlife reserves.

Great rivers such as the Kaveri, the Krishna and the Godavari rise in the Western Ghats and flow eastward to drain into the Bay of Bengal, while the relatively shorter westward-flowing rivers create beautiful scenery including huge waterfalls, dense forests and large lakes in Kerala and Karnataka.

The Deccan Plateau lies between the Western Ghats and the Eastern Ghats, a less dramatic chain comprising massive blocks of hills less than 1,500m (5,000ft) high in interrupted stretches through Andhra and Tamil Nadu. Consisting of some of the world's oldest rocks and layers of lava from ancient volcanic eruptions, the Deccan is veined by rivers such as the Tungabhadra and Krishna that gave rise to the great empires of Andhra and Karnataka. Beyond the slopes of the plateau, the east coast is an affluent area, with the ports of Chennai and Vishakhapatnam, and fertile deltas. The southeast coast has significant mangrove forests that are nurseries for marine life, as well as being important areas for birdlife.

Economy

The most significant development in the economy of Southern India in the last 20 years has been the IT boom. As well as Indian software companies, multinationals attracted by the qualified yet relatively inexpensive technical expertise of the region, have invested in software development companies in Bangalore, Hyderabad, Chennai and other cities. The engineering industries of Tamil Nadu, Karnataka and Andhra have also seen a boom with the growing demand for aircraft, cars, trains and machinery in India's rising economy, with growth curbed only slightly by the financial crisis. Other important industries are leather-tanning in Chennai, textile mills in Coimbatore, hosiery at Tirupur, chemicals and fertilisers, sugar mills and mining.

While the IT boom has been an urban phenomenon, the bedrock of the local economy is agriculture, with Kerala growing much of India's rubber, spices, lemon grass, coconuts, tapioca and cocoa. Tea and coffee plantations thrive in the Western Ghats, while the river plains, deltas and coastal areas produce rice, sugar cane, groundnuts and other oilseeds, and cotton. Fishing is another important revenue source.

History

10th–5th centuries BC	Megalithic sites show that a sophisticated civilisation has existed in Kerala for centuries.
3rd century BC	The Cheras, Cholas and Pandyas rule Southern India.
1st century AD	Thomas the Apostle is believed to have visited Kerala in AD 52 and introduced Christianity. Jews land at Muziris in about AD 70.
2nd and 3rd centuries	The Buddhist architecture of the Satavahana rulers of Andhra reaches its apogee. Tamil Sangam literature, which flourished in the early Christian era, offers an insight into socio-economics and culture in Kerala under the Chera kings.
6th and 7th centuries	Malik Ibn Dinar, a disciple of Muhammad, brings Islam to Kerala, and establishes one of the first mosques in India in the 7th century AD. The Chalukya dynasties thrive in Karnataka.
7th century	The Pallava ruler Narasimhavarman makes Mahabalipuram (Mamallapuram) famous as a port.
9th century	A new Chera dynasty emerges. *Perumal*, or ruler, was the sovereign power, but people's rights were acknowledged by the presence of elected representatives. Malayalam emerges as a distinct language.
10th and 11th centuries	The Chola rulers of the neighbouring Tamil Coromandel coast bring an end to Chera sovereignty in 1102.
13th–15th centuries	The Islamic conquerors of Northern India make incursions into Southern India. Vijayanagar rulers respond by amalgamating into a kingdom at Hampi.
1498–1502	Vasco da Gama makes landfall near Kozhikode.
16th century	The Deccan Sultanates dominate Karnataka and great monuments are built at Bidar and Bijapur.

17th century	Mughal Aurangzeb extends his empire into Southern India. The Marathas extend their rule to Central Tamil Nadu.
1604	A Dutch alliance with the Zamorin begins a joint effort to displace the Portuguese in Kerala.
1653	Syrian Christians revolt against Portuguese attempts to Latinise the church, a turning point in the history of Syrian Christianity.
1663	The Dutch succeed in displacing the Portuguese from Kochi, Cranganore, Kollam, Alleppey and Cannanore.
1761–99	The Sultans of Mysore dominate Karnataka and make incursions into Kerala.
1795	The British seize the Dutch fort at Kochi.
1800	The British subjugate Kerala and divide it into the British province of Malabar, and the princely states of Kochi and Travancore.
1805	After a five-year struggle against the British, Pazhassi Raja dies in battle and is given a hero's funeral.
1812	Forces are called in to crush the tribal revolt against collecting taxes in cash instead of in kind.
1836–56	Tensions between the Hindu landlords and Muslim tenants result in the Mappilla Riots.
1885	The Indian National Congress is formed and instigates talks with the British.
1919	Kerala's committee of the National Congress is convened at Trichur.
1947	India gains independence and northern Kerala becomes part of Madras State.
1956	Southern India is reorganised into the states of Tamil Nadu, Andhra Pradesh, Kerala and Mysore (later renamed Karnataka).
1957– 2010	For more on recent political developments, *see p11.*

Politics

As a country of considerable religious diversity, India has sustained a constitutional democratic system for more than 60 years in the face of tremendous pressure and challenges, with the possible exception of two years (1975–7) when Indira Gandhi, as prime minister, imposed a state of emergency, banning political activity. Key features of the constitution include secularism, equal rights for women, universal suffrage, human rights and the abolition of the caste system.

India's government

India is a sovereign democratic republic, and every citizen 18 years of age or over is eligible to vote. The president is the official head but exercises power under the authority of the prime minister and council.

The *Lok Sabha* (House of the People) consists of up to 552 members, with 530 members representing the 28 states, up to 20 members representing the Union Territories, and two members of the Anglo-Indian Community to be nominated by the president, if the community is not already adequately represented in the House. The upper house, *Rajya Sabha* (Council of States), has 12 members nominated by the president and 238 members elected by the state assemblies and union territories.

The 29 states have legislative assemblies with the governor as the official head nominated by the president, and the chief minister and cabinet responsible for the actual administration. Like the central government, most of the states have two houses of parliament.

The central government controls the armed forces, aviation, railways, postal services, currency and international affairs. The state governments are responsible for industry, agriculture, roads, forestry and environment, and internal security.

The political scene in India

Congress Party leader Jawaharlal Nehru became the first prime minister of India in 1947, and Congress has won the majority of the general elections held in the country. At the 11th general elections, in 1996, Congress was defeated by the Bharatiya Janta Party (BJP), which has won the elections twice since then.

With an unprecedented boom in the economy in the early 2000s, BJP launched the 'India Shining' campaign which focused on their achievements in increased exports, technological progress, image building, tourism and

IT, but this was effectively countered by the Congress Party which appealed to the rural masses and won the 2004 elections, with Dr Manmohan Singh becoming prime minister. He and his party were returned to power in 2009.

Politics in Southern India

Regional political parties have been strong forces in the elections of Southern India. Tamil Nadu's elections have been dominated alternately by the DMK from 1967, when it defeated the Congress Party, and AIADMK, which split from the main DMK body in 1972. During the 2006 elections, DMK was elected to power with its head, M Karunanidhi, as chief minister, beating the AIADMK whose chief, J Jayalalitha, had a long spell as chief minister of Tamil Nadu.

In Andhra, Telugu Desam, formed by N T Rama Rao, dominated the elections in the 1980s. In 1994, N Chandrababu Naidu, who succeeded N T Rama Rao, brought in a technological revolution, making Hyderabad one of the software capitals of India. However, the Congress Party won the 2004 elections, with Y S Rajashekhara Reddy as chief minister. The party has since gone on to win several more local elections. For over four decades, there have been calls for the region of Telangana, which includes Hyderabad, to be made an independent state. Momentum has grown, and in late 2009 the Indian government approved the move. However, it quickly backtracked, saying that such a change first required all-party consensus, and statehood for Telangana now seems to be on hold.

Kerala is unique in having elected the Communist Party of India in 1957, when the first legislative assembly was formed for the state. But Communist dominance of the political scene suffered a blow in 2009 when the Congress Party emerged victorious from the parliamentary election.

Karnataka's politics have been largely dominated by the Congress Party, but in 2006 the JD(S)-BJP coalition was elected into power. B S Yeddyurappa was appointed chief minister in November 2007. The BJP was also victorious in the general election of 2009.

Government Museum, Chennai

Culture

Despite its long history of global maritime contact and European colonisation, Kerala has retained its distinctive cultural identity. For many visitors to Kerala, its tolerant culture, embracing Hinduism, Judaism, Christianity and Islam, is a particular attraction, and this is reflected in the state's dance and drama, as well as in the martial arts and alternative medicine.

The caste system

Brahmins are at the apex of the Hindu caste system, which is a system of inherited social groupings within the society. Traditionally Brahmins have been priests and learned people, but today they are seen in various professions, although they generally follow rules of conduct such as strict vegetarianism.

The Nairs have been a dominant force in the political and social life of Kerala for a long time. They followed a matrilineal system of inheritance that many believe has its origins in the 10th and 11th centuries when Nair warriors went to battle against the Cholas. This practice became illegal in 1956 when the Hindu Succession Act gave equal rights of inheritance to men and women.

Traditionally, Nairs lived in community homes called *Tharawads*, which were designed to house the extended family. Women lived with their brothers and sisters, and their children, with shared kitchens and dining areas. Between 50 and 80 people often shared a large courtyard house called a *Nalakettu*.

Usually landowners, Nairs are credited with the preservation of the Kallaripayattu martial arts and the Kathakali dance drama. The Nairs continue to influence politics and have formed the Nair Service Society to promote their aims and aspirations.

With such good literacy and political awareness, there has been a tremendous backlash against the caste system in parts of India, especially concerning untouchability, and the domination of the upper castes has declined.

Tribes and nomadic groups

With Southern India's high literacy rate, many tribes have seen improved standards of living, but some tribal villages still subsist on marginal agriculture and on gathering forest produce such as honey, and they have retained their traditional lifestyles. The main tribal groups – travellers of the Malayarayan, Mannan, Muthuvan, Oorali, Paliyan, Hill Pulayan, Malapandaram, Ulladan, Malayan, Paniya and Adiya – are likely to meet near tourist destinations, especially in the Idukki and Wayanad Districts. Todas near Ooty (*see pp138–9*) in Tamil Nadu live in igloo-like bamboo and grass huts and wear brightly patterned shawls. Other tribal groups include the Kotas, who have a musical tradition; the Kurumbas, who have mostly taken employment at plantations; and the Irulas, known for their snake-catching skills. The Lambanis and other groups of Banjaras are semi-nomadic groups that are known for their embroidery skills in Andhra and Karnataka. Andhra has a number of tribal groups, most of them concentrated in the hills around Araku (*see p141*).

Language

The four principal languages of Southern India are Malayalam spoken in Kerala, Tamil in Tamil Nadu, Kannada in Karnataka and Telugu in Andhra Pradesh. All of these have Dravidian roots with some Sanskrit influences. Konkani is spoken along the coast of Karnataka. Dakhani and Urdu, languages that developed from an amalgamation of Indian languages and those of Islamic invaders such as Arabic, Persian and Turkish, are widely spoken in Hyderabad and some other historic cities of Andhra and Karnataka. French is still spoken by some of the residents of Pondicherry (*see pp112–13*), which is now a Union Territory. English is widely spoken in Southern India, especially in the cities of Chennai, Bangalore, Hyderabad, Kochi and Thiruvananthapuram.

Music and dance

See pp58–9.

Hindu paintings on a house in Kollam, Kerala

Religion

The vivid depictions of multi-limbed deities can leave the visitor in no doubt that Hinduism is the prominent faith in Southern India. However, pockets of other believers can be found: a fifth of Keralans are Christian, and both the north of that state and the Andhra Pradesh capital Hyderabad have a visible Islamic influence. Wherever you go in the region, all the religions practised have left an eye-popping architectural legacy, with temples of all hues, churches and mosques among the most striking constructions.

Hinduism

Hinduism is a religious tradition with ancient roots dating back to the third and second millennia BC. With no founder, prophet or church-like organisation to define the rules, Hinduism has embraced new features and a diversity of religious beliefs even up until recent times. The holy books of the Hindus are the *Vedas* (incorporating the *Upanishads* as the final volumes), which are often considered the foundation of Indian philosophy, with epics like the *Ramayana* and *Mahabharata*, and the *Bhagavad Gita* which is based on the philosophies of Lord Krishna as they were related to warrior prince Arjun in an episode of the *Mahabharata*.

Hindus believe in a cycle of reincarnation determined by their *karma*, the consequences of former actions that can flow into the next life. The aims of a Hindu are to attain material wealth honestly (*artha*), satisfy all desires (*kama*) and perform all duties (*dharma*), all of which will lead, through good *karma*, to *moksha*, liberation from the endless rebirth cycle.

An aspect of Hinduism that most visitors to India find hard to understand is the multitude of gods and goddesses. Actually, most of them are incarnations and manifestations of a few, and this may be the result of Hinduism incorporating regional beliefs into its pantheon. Three Gods are considered integral to Hinduism: Brahma as the creator, Vishnu as the preserver of the universe (usually worshipped as one of his many incarnations that rids the world of destroying forces like demons) and Shiva, the destroyer, who is worshipped in many forms, such as Natraja when he dances to destroy evil. The consort of Brahma is Sarasvati, the goddess of learning. Vishnu's consort Lakshmi is worshipped as the goddess of wealth, and Shiva's consort Parvati has many manifestations, including Durga and Kali, goddesses of power and destruction. Most Hindus start a new venture by worshipping Ganesh, the elephant-headed son of Lord Shiva, who is said to bring luck, knowledge and prosperity.

Some key features of Hindu religious traditions are *darshan* (visions), which denote the importance of visiting holy places, *puja* or ritualistic worship, and cremation of the dead.

From the 8th century, the *Bhakti* tradition or devotional form of Hinduism emerged in Southern India and became popular in the rest of the country as well. This was a period of resurgence for Hinduism, as Buddhism and Jainism were becoming dominant in Southern India, and saw poet saints converting kingdoms such as Madurai from Jainism to Hinduism. Some of the songs of the Tamil poet saints are still sung. Leaders such as Sankaracharya brought in a resurgence of Hinduism in Kerala.

Christianity

It is widely believed by the Christians of Kerala that one of Christ's Apostles, St Thomas, settled in Malabar in AD 52 and introduced Christianity to Kerala. In AD 345, a Christian Syrian merchant named Thomas landed on the Kerala coast and preached Christianity based on the practices of the Syrian Church. In the 9th century a number of Christians from Syria settled in Kerala, and this led to the Christians of Kerala calling themselves Syrian Christians.

The Portuguese promoted Roman Catholic practices, but the Syrian Christians resented the Latinisation of their Church and took the Oath of the Coonan Cross separating their Church from Rome. In 1662, however, many of the Syrian churches reunited with Rome.

The Dutch were not very tolerant of the Portuguese Roman Catholic

The nave of St Francis Church in Kochi, possibly the oldest European church in India (*see p49*)

Religion

practices and they converted churches, like that of St Francis in Kochi, into their own Protestant ones. The British introduced the Anglican Church, and among its members were the Syrian Jacobite Group.

The most important pilgrimage for the majority of Christians in Southern India is to Our Lady of Health, Vailankani. The shrine was established in Tamil Nadu in the 17th century following a series of miracles and apparitions. It attracts a large crowd of worshippers, including non-Christians.

Islam

Islam began in Mecca around the 7th century when the Prophet Muhammad compiled revelations from Allah, and was brought to Kerala in the same century by one of the Prophet's followers, Malik Ibn Dinar.

However, the history of Islam in Southern India is generally attributed to trade with the Middle East. The religion found a tolerant society, and the support of Hindu princes, like the Zamorins of Kozhikode, helped Islam grow in Kerala. Islamic contact grew as the Arabs gained a monopoly over trade between the Zamorin-dominated Malabar Coast and the Mediterranean.

To be a Muslim is to accept the fact that there is no god but Allah, and Muhammad is his prophet. This simple principle of Islam, submission to god, is called *shahada* and is the bedrock of the belief. By uttering these words, a Muslim commits to a life of praise-giving obedience to god. The *Qur'an* is the holy book of the Muslims and the supreme authority on the Islamic faith. The five pillars of Islam are the profession of faith regarding the one God and Muhammad as God's messenger, worship five times daily, almsgiving, fasting in the month of Ramadan, and the pilgrimage to Mecca. Alcohol and pork are prohibited and meat must be prepared in a way called *halal* that involves draining the blood of an animal while it is alive. Gambling and charging interest on loans are forbidden.

Judaism

There are ancient accounts of Jewish contacts with Kerala. Some refer back to trade with King Solomon, escaping injustice in Assyria, fleeing slavery in Babylon or the destruction of Jerusalem. Referred to as 'Black Jews', they were later supplemented by the 'White Jews' fleeing the Inquisitions of Spain and Portugal in the 16th century, and later again by Ashkenazi Jews escaping the pogroms. The Jews were influential merchants, and in the 10th and 11th centuries a Jewish merchant, Joseph Rabban, was granted royal privileges by Bhaskara Ravi Varma. The Raja of Kochi gave similar grants when Jews moved to Kochi after the near-destruction of the community by the Arabs in Malabar, and Portuguese persecution. Today, only a few Jewish families remain in Kochi after the mass migration to Israel in the 1950s.

Buddhism

Buddhism is based on the beliefs of
Siddhartha Gautama Buddha who was
born into a princely family in the 6th
century BC. His preaching is often
regarded as a reaction to Hinduism,
accepting the doctrine of reincarnation
and the law of *karma*, but rejecting the
concept of a pantheon of gods and the
caste system.

Once popular in Southern India,
Buddhism declined after the *Bhakti*
movement of Hinduism in the 8th
century. Some of the most significant
relics can be seen in Andhra Pradesh.
Tibetan settlements in Karnataka, most
of them in Kodagu district (*see pp94–5*),
have established Buddhist monasteries
near Bylakuppe including Namdroling,
known as the Golden Temple.

Jainism

Jainism is based on the teachings of
Mahavira, one of the 24 *tirthankaras*
(ford-makers) sacred to Jains. The key
features of the Jain religion are
liberation from the wheel of rebirth
and the belief that all life is sacred.
Strict vegetarianism is a feature of
Jainism, for Jains believe that even the
smallest life form has a soul.

There is now only a small Jain
population in Southern India,
including migrants from Rajasthan
and Gujarat, but there are historic
Jain temples and monastic caves in
Karnataka and Kerala, as well as
living temples in most cities. An
important pilgrimage for Jains is to
Sravanabelagola (*see pp92–3*) with its
colossal statue.

Jain pilgrims giving offerings at the base of the Gomateshvara statue, Sravanabelagola

Festivals

Nowhere is the colour and clamour of Southern India so graphically encapsulated as in its dazzling festivals. Naturally, religion is at the heart of many celebrations, with droves of the devout turning up to enjoy elephantine convoys, vibrant costumes and invigorating musical accompaniment. There is also secular fun to be had, with Kerala's backwater boat races being an exciting case in point. Cultural festivals centring on dance, drama, music, art and food are another burgeoning branch of events.

Pongal

Around 14 January

Pongal is a Tamil harvest festival, coinciding with Makar Sankranti which is celebrated in the rest of India. Cows are decorated and processions can be seen on the streets of the state during the festival, and floor paintings are created outside many houses.

Sabarimala Festival

January

This is one of Kerala's most important festivals honouring Ayyappan, whom devotees believe to be born from the union of Shiva and Vishnu's female form Mohini. Dressed in black, devotees make the pilgrimage to Sabarimala with stops for ceremonies along the way. Ascending the 18 steps to the temple, they promise to bring an end to sin.

Thaipusam

January–February

This festival honours Subramanya or Karthikeyan, the God of War, at his temples in Kerala. This god has six heads denoting the five senses and the mind, and is depicted on a peacock.

Mannanam Convention

February

From 1894, this convention has been held in honour of Father Chavara, who is buried here and who is considered to be a saint because of his work with the lower classes. Since then it has grown to become one of Asia's largest Christian Conventions.

Krishna Festival at Guruvayoor

February–March

This ten-day festival is celebrated with processions of elephants. The Krishna image is carried on top of an elephant during the last day's procession, before it is bathed in the temple tank. Ritual bathing is a feature of the festival, as devotees want to share the water with the deity.

www.guruvayurkrishnatemple.com

Shivratri

February–March

Maha Shivratri commemorates the night when Shiva danced the *Tandava*, dance of destruction, and is celebrated with feasting, fairs and devotional rituals. Fairs take place at Alwaye and Attappady. *www.mahashivratri.org*

Painkuni Festival at Thiruvananthapuram

March–April

This is a ten-night festival at the Padmanabhaswamy Temple, ending with a procession that carries the idol on an elephant to the sea for ritual bathing.

Pooram

April–May

This festival is a magnificent spectacle at Thrissur, with elephants, decorated with gold, carrying beautiful parasols, and paraded to the accompaniment of drumming and firework displays.

Onam

August–September

The most important festival in Kerala, Onam celebrates the harvest and the reign of philanthropic King Mahabali. The celebrations are spectacular at Alappuzha, where boat races take place, and at Thrissur, where you can enjoy the elephant processions.

Chandanakkudham Mahotsava

October

This festival is celebrated with sword play, singing, dancing, processions, elephant parades and fireworks at Beemapalli near Thiruvananthapuram. Muslims carry incense sticks to the tomb of Bheema Beevi, a woman pilgrim who travelled to Mecca and was said to have divine powers.

Other festivals include: the Nishagandhi Dance Festival (February), the food festival at Thiruvananthapuram (April), the Surusa Drama Festival in Kozhikode (May), the Chembai Music Festival in Thiruvananthapuram (September), the Mysore Dasara (September or October), the Hampi Festival (November), the Kerala Kalamandalam Festival at Cheruthuruthy (December and January) and the Ashtamudi Craft and Art Festival at Kollam (December and January).

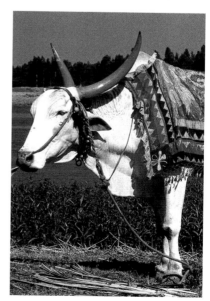

Colourful decorations for Pongal

Festivals

Impressions

Southern India, covering the states of Kerala, Karnataka, Tamil Nadu and Andhra Pradesh, plus the Union Territory of Pondicherry, is a vast area. You will find varied and beautiful scenery, architectural gems including some of India's greatest temples, forts and palaces, wildlife reserves and traditions of fine arts, music, dance, handicrafts, literature and Ayurvedic medicine.

Architecture

While most studies of Southern India's architecture focus on the religious monuments, there are also excellent examples of domestic architecture, such as the mansions of the Chettiars of Tamil Nadu (*see p117*), some of which tourists can now visit, and the Nair houses of Kerala. Great forts were built at Golconda near Hyderabad, with canal systems and water storage facilities able to withstand a siege.

The prosperity of the Nizam of Hyderabad and the Maharaja of Mysore, the two most affluent princely states in all of India, also saw great palaces built in Mysore (*see pp88–9*) and Hyderabad (*see pp120–21*). These palaces blended Hindu, Islamic and European styles of architecture in the late 19th and early 20th centuries, at a time when peace treaties between the British and the princes ushered in a period of flamboyance.

The European powers dominated Southern India from the 17th century,

and relics of colonial rule include the French buildings of Pondicherry town on the Tamil coast, Yanam town near the Andhra coast and Mahe on the Kerala coast. Dutch and Portuguese influences can be seen in the buildings of Kerala, while the British influence is evident in the impressive buildings of Chennai and Bangalore, as well as the colonial bungalows at hill stations such as Ooty and Munnar.

It is, however, the rich heritage of religious architecture that draws many travellers to Southern India.

Buddhist *stupas* of Andhra

Stupas are hemispherical structures that evolved from simple burial mounds into elaborate monuments. They usually consist of a carved gateway called a *torana*, railings around an enclosure and platforms called *vedica*, carved pillars, *chattrayashti*, which is a parasol or canopy, and an ambulatory. The ambulatory is provided for the ritual of *pradakshina*, or clockwise circumambulation, transporting the worshipper into a magical force field of divine realms. The hemispherical dome represents the sacred hill or axis linking heaven with earth, while the square platform, conical spire, crescent moon and circular disc represent cosmic elements that have symbolic significance. The Satavahana rulers

Sri Meenakshi, Madurai

built intricate *stupas* in Andhra Pradesh that can be seen at Nagarjunakonda (*see pp126–7*) and Amravati (*see p128*).

Temples

The Hindu temple design works on principles laid down by priests in manuals called *Shastras* that set out in detail everything from the building process to the layout and the symbolic significance of the elevations. The temple focuses on the sanctum as the home of the presiding deity, with a succession of halls or buildings leading to it for the worshippers to assemble in or move through for *darshan* (beholding) of the deity. Hindu architecture uses beams and columns for support. The Dravida temple architecture (*see p100*) evolved from the 6th century to the 17th century in Tamil Nadu and has distinctive features such as the *gopurams* or towering gates and pyramidal towering roofs. The Hoysala dynasty's temples in Karnataka have their own distinctive style of a star-shaped plinth with an ambulatory around the temple, and the hall inside has beautifully carved columns.

Mosques

The mosques and mausoleum complexes of northern Karnataka and western Andhra Pradesh are in the Indo-Islamic style, inspired by the Turkish and other Middle-Eastern roots of the Islamic rulers, but incorporating elements of the artistry of the Hindu craftsmen.

Culture shock

Despite a high literacy rate and quality of life by Indian standards, Kerala has a number of shocks for first-time visitors, such as crowds, poverty, dust, dirt and disease. Although most people in Kerala, at least in the south of the state, are used to tourists, do not be surprised if visitors from other states or residents of out-of-the-way places stare, crowd around, giggle and involve you in inane conversation out of curiosity. It is perfectly common in India to discuss personal matters, politics and religion, and you will often be asked about your family and income.

Bureaucratic hurdles, slow service, crowded roads and long queues can try your patience, as elsewhere in India.

Conduct

Body language

The most common greeting in India is palms joined together as in prayer, accompanied by a *namaste* (reverential bow). Shaking hands is becoming a common form of greeting in India, but only the most westernised Indians will shake hands with a woman. The right hand is used for eating, receiving and giving.

Religious etiquette

Despite an amazing religious and cultural diversity, etiquette is similar for most religious places in Kerala. You will have to take off your shoes to visit temples, mosques and churches, while smoking and shows of affection are considered disrespectful at all religious places. You should also dress modestly and not talk loudly in temples and mosques. Touching idols at temples may be prohibited. Some Hindu temples in Kerala, especially those in the southern districts, do not allow foreigners to enter the sanctuary.

Women travellers

Outside popular tourist destinations, Indians are unaccustomed to foreigners, and they may stare or pass rude comments if they see western

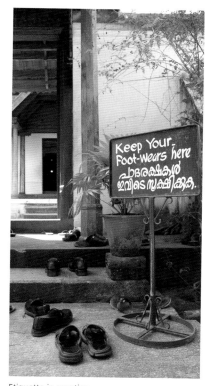

Etiquette in practice

women in bathing clothes. Away from the beaches and swimming pools, women are expected to dress modestly and not wear bikinis, swimsuits, shorts and skimpy skirts. Most Indian women do not drink or smoke.

Holidays

India celebrates many holidays during which monuments, museums, banks and shops may not be open.

Photography

Southern India is extremely photogenic, with lush hills, pretty beaches, picturesque villages, historic cities, beautiful temples and other monuments, and an abundance of wildlife. Sunny weather most of the year adds to the joy of photography in Kerala and the rest of Southern India.

It is generally better to ask before you take photographs of local people, especially women. Taking them without permission is considered rude by some, although many Indians are keen to be photographed. Children trying to get into the frame or curious people wanting to see your equipment could crowd you.

Although taking the necessary equipment with you can save time, many shops stock extra memory cards, and at the main tourist sites hawkers walk around selling such supplies.

Camera thefts are common in India. Always take care of your camera, and as far as it is possible do not leave it in a hotel room or taxi.

Kerala

Forming a strip of land along the southwest coast of India, Kerala is home to a wide diversity of scenery within its narrow confines, including some of Southern India's finest beaches, the backwaters immediately inland, spice-planted midlands and the tropical forests of the Western Ghats that rise inland parallel to the coast. Its colourful cultural life and welcoming people also add to the charm.

The spices of Kerala attracted traders, invaders and settlers to its harbours, and these influences are reflected in the state's many historic buildings. The temples of Thiruvananthapuram (Trivandrum), the state capital, are in the Dravida style of the Cholas who conquered Kerala in the 10th and 11th centuries, while its museums and public buildings were designed by British architects. Many of Kochi's buildings show the influences of the Portuguese, Dutch and British colonial powers, and the town is also home to the oldest intact synagogue and one of the oldest churches in Southern India. The influence of trade with the Arabs can be seen in the Islamic quarters of Kozhikode, Kannur and Kasaragod. Kerala's own distinct identity is best explored in its heartland – Kottayam district, with its Syrian Christian churches, wooden plantation houses and beautifully painted Keralan temples, and Thrissur district, which has holy temples as well as a number of

important institutions for the dance dramas of Kerala and the classical music of Southern India.

For decades, chartered flights have landed at Thiruvananthapuram because of its proximity to Kovalam, which is now seeing an upmarket renewal with luxury resorts developing along its beaches, as well as further south at Chowara and Poovar. North of Thiruvananthapuram, the historic towns of Kollam, Alappuzha and Kottayam offer access to the backwaters, a special attraction of Kerala. These are navigable waterways that pass through a lush green landscape of plantations, villages, fishermen and waterfront markets. For many travellers, a night on board a houseboat, or a sunset boat trip, is a highlight of their stay.

The stretch of coast north of Kochi is less visited than the southern one, but it is now seeing more development, with resorts growing up along the beaches and backwaters near the great fort of Bekal, the historic city of Kozhikode and the historic town of Kannur.

Running parallel to the coast, the Western Ghats are richly forested and are also planted with tea, coffee and spices. One of the most popular destinations in these hills is Periyar Lake, where tigers, elephants, sloth bears, wild dogs and other wildlife come to drink. Munnar, the main hill resort of Kerala, is about 1,500m (5,000ft) above sea level amid a dramatic landscape of tea plantations, high peaks, stunningly beautiful lakes and wildlife-rich forests.

In the past, the barrier formed by the Western Ghats protected much of Kerala from invaders, with the exception of aggressors from Tamil Nadu and Karnataka, who entered through the Palghat (or Palakkad) Gap. Near the Gap are the rainforests of the Silent Valley and the Annamalai hills. The hills of the Wayanad district across the Gap are the setting for attractive waterfalls and wildlife reserves that are contiguous with those of Karnataka and Tamil Nadu.

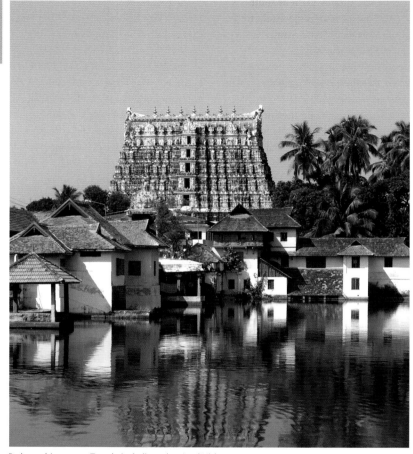

Padmanabhaswamy Temple is dedicated to Lord Vishnu

THIRUVANANTHAPURAM
Thiruvananthapuram city

As Indian state capitals go, Thiruvananthapuram comes as a breath of fresh air. In part this can be taken literally – its tropical atmosphere gives it a lushness that is a marked departure from much of arid India, if you are flying in from out of state. The tropical humidity has also fostered a more relaxed pace of life, with little in the way of urban franticness. Another boon is its small size, making the town easily navigable and not as overwhelming as many of the larger cities. The main attractions are all in close proximity, with the obvious exception of the beach – but sunseekers in Kerala would usually be heading north or south, to Varkala or Kovalam respectively, to satisfy their sand lust anyway.

With a history dating back to the medieval Venadu dynasty, nobility permeates the development of Thiruvananthapuram, once the capital of the princely state of Travancore. It takes its rather lengthy name from the Sanskrit and Malayalam for 'abode of Lord Ananta', a serpent deity. For none-too-opaque reasons, the city is often referred to by its British-era name of Trivandrum, especially by foreigners.

Compared with the beach resorts close by, the Keralan capital is particularly rich in cultural attractions, a legacy of its illustrious past. Grand temples, palaces and the remains of the fort are offset by lower-key winding back alleys, still peppered by old-school businesses. There's also a complex that is home to two museums, an art gallery and zoological gardens, allowing you to 'do' much of the tourist trail in one fell swoop.

Thiruvananthapuram is 220km (137 miles) from Kochi and 382km (237 miles) from Kozhikode, with good rail connections with Madgaon (Goa) and other parts of India. Thiruvananthapuram also has an international airport. The tourist office is at Park View near the museums.

KALARIPAYATTU

This martial art is said to have evolved during the battles between the Cheras and the Cholas in the 9th and the 12th centuries. The *Kalaripayattu* martial techniques became popular in the 12th century when feudal lords of the principalities that comprised medieval Kerala were constantly at war with each other. Arenas called *kalaris* were set up to train warriors for combat (*payattu* is the Malayalam word for combat). Each village had a *kalari*, near the local temple and sacred pond, which ensured a combination of health, fitness, defence, religion and hygiene. The *kalari* itself comprised a gymnasium, a temple and educational facilities. A trainer, called the *Gurukkal*, was responsible for the martial training, education and health of each member of the *kalari*. Training was so effective in producing skilled warriors that the British banned the *kalari* system in 1792, and the practice of *Kalaripayattu* had almost died out by the 19th century.

Training traditionally begins at the age of eight and can continue for a decade. Students are trained in the art of using wooden weapons such as the *cheruvate* (a short stick), *kettukara* (long stick) and *ottakal* (a wooden club). *Ankatari* is the technique of duelling with metal weapons, including swords, shields, spears and daggers. The most dreaded *kalari* weapon is the *umurio* sword, and training in the use of this sword is generally given only to a potential *Gurukkal*, as it is a lethal weapon.

Oil massages, traditionally used to increase the suppleness of the body, have now developed into a branch of Ayurveda. The martial art sequences of *Kalaripayattu* are said to have been adopted into the martial arts of other countries.

At Thiruvananthapuram's CVN Kalari (*Tel: 0471 247 4182. www.cvnkalarikerala.com*), the *Gurukkal* trains students in armed and unarmed combat. The Kalari welcomes visitors and can arrange demonstrations.

Thiruvananthapuram

Arts and Crafts Museum

Formerly the Napier Museum, this government museum opened in 1856. The colourful façade has European, Indo-Saracenic, Keralan and Chinese Pagoda features. Inside is an excellent collection of 12th-century bronzes, 15th-century woodcarvings, temple chariots, gold jewellery, Javanese objects, Kathakali figures and a model of the Guruvayur Temple. To the east is the **Natural History Museum**, which houses a model of a Nair *Tharawad* (wood and stucco house), and explains each part of a *Nalakettu*, a traditional courtyard house of Kerala.
Open: Tue, Thur–Sun 10am–4.45pm, Wed 1–4.45pm. Admission charge.

Botanical and Zoological Park

Established in 1859, this park is worth visiting for its zoo, which is one of the largest in India. The botanical garden has many interesting trees and plants.
Off Museum Road, Palayam. Tel: 0471 231 6275. museumzoo@sancharnet.in. Open: Tue–Sun 9am–6.15pm. Admission charge.

Connemara Market

This market has a granite entrance and overhanging roofs supported by brackets.

Padmanabhaswamy Temple

Raja Marthanda Varma rebuilt this temple in 1733, and it is said to house an idol found in the hills around Thiruvananthapuram. Unusually for Kerala, the architecture is predominantly Dravidian, with an intricately carved seven-storeyed *gopuram* (towering gatehouse) behind a temple tank. The interior of the temple is usually open only to Hindus, but foreign visitors can request permission to visit in order to see the murals, sculptures and the columns supporting the main pavilions. The central shrine has images of Vishnu, Brahma and Shiva. *1km (²/₃ mile) southwest of Trivandrum Central Station. Tel: 0471 245 0233. Open: daily 4.15–5.15am, 6.45–7.30am, 8.30–10.30am, 11.30–11.45am & 5.15–7.30pm (not officially open to non-Hindus). If granted permission to enter, visitors are required to wear white sarongs (dhotis) for men and sarees for women.*

Puthe Maliga Palace Museum

Sometimes pronounced Puthen Malika Palace and also called Kuthira Maliga Palace, this building was built in the 19th century by Maharajah Swami Tirunal. The name is derived from the frieze of wooden horses and literally means the 'palace of horses'. Made from teak and rosewood, with granite columns and marble interiors, the palace houses music halls, reading rooms, an excellent library, European mirrors and chandeliers, weapons, crystal and ivory thrones, Kathakali idols, elephant *howdahs* (seats laid across elephant backs) and other princely memorabilia. The palace is also renowned for hosting a classical music festival in January or February each year. *Immediately to the east of Padmanabhaswamy Temple, or 900m (¹/₂ mile) southwest of Trivandrum Central Station. Tel: 0471 247 3952. Open: Mon–Sat 8.30am–1pm, 3–5.30pm. Small admission charge.*

Sri Chitra Art Gallery

This gallery exhibits a collection of Raja Ravi Varma's portraiture, as well as a variety of works of Rajasthani, Tanjore, Balinese, Mughal, Chinese, Japanese, Tibetan Buddhist and South Indian art. *Off Museum Road, Palayam. Open: Tue, Thur–Sun 10am–4.45pm, Wed 1–4.45pm. Admission charge.*

St Joseph's Cathedral

This 19th-century cathedral is one of the oldest churches in Thiruvananthapuram, with a tall tower and a red-brick façade showing Gothic influences. The church has some interesting British tombstones to the rear. *MG Road, close to the stadium. Tel: 0471 232 0132. Services in English at 5.45am daily.*

RAVI VARMA'S PAINTINGS

Raja Ravi Varma (1848–1906) was one of India's first artists to take up oil painting, to master perspective and to use human models for Hindu deities. He was awarded the Vira Sanghala Decoration by the state of Travancore.

Thiruvananthapuram environs

Situated along the coast where the Western Ghats come fairly close to the sea, Thiruvananthapuram is the starting point for trips to lesser-known beaches and minor hill stations. The excursions are good options for those who want to get away from the crowds of the state capital and the travellers' scene at nearby Kovalam (*see p32*). Thiruvananthapuram is also a good base for trips south to Tamil Nadu.

Kariavattom

North of Thiruvananthapuram, Kariavattom is home to **Kerala University** and the **Technopark**, one of India's largest computing, electronics and industrial parks. The **University Library** (*www.keralauniversity.edu. Usually open from 10am–4pm Mon–Fri except during the university's holidays*) has a superb collection of palm-leaf manuscripts in numerous languages, besides copper inscriptions and paper manuscripts, initiated by the Travancore Princely State.
15km (9 miles) from Thiruvananthapuram.

Nedumangad

The renovated **Koyikkal Palace** at Nedumangad has a folklore museum containing musical instruments and folk arts, and a fine coin collection.
About 18km (11 miles) north of Thiruvananthapuram. Tel: 0472 281 2136. Open: Tue–Sun 9am–5pm. Admission charge.

Neyyar Lake

Neyyar Lake is the focal point of the 128sq km (49sq mile) **Neyyar Wildlife Sanctuary** (*Tel: 0471 232 2217. wildlife@sify.com. Open: Tue–Sun 9am–4pm. Admission charge*). Here you are likely to see elephants, tigers, bears, gaur, deer and wild boar, but be warned – they are hard to spot. The higher ranges are covered by grassland inhabited by the tahr (a goat-like mammal) and other herbivores, but trekking permits are essential. There is a lion safari park, where some lions can be seen in an enclosure, and a crocodile park.

The **Sivananda Yoga Vendanta Dhanwantari Ashram** (*Tel: 0471 227 3093. guestindia@sivananda.org*) overlooks Neyyar Lake and conducts yoga classes for beginners, advanced students and teachers. The Agastya Hills, some of the highest in southern Kerala at 1,869m (6,130ft), can be seen from the lake on a clear day.
About 32km (20 miles) east of Thiruvananthapuram. Buses leave from the KSRTC Thampanoor stand in Thiruvananthapuram.

Padmanabhapuram Palace

This seat of power of Travancore State is now officially in Tamil Nadu. The name refers to the lotus emerging from the navel of Lord Vishnu to whom this palace was dedicated by Raja Marthanda Varma. The residence and administrative headquarters of the Venadu dynasty before they moved to

Thiruvananthapuram in 1750, the oldest parts probably date from the 1550s. Built from teak and supported by granite, it is an excellent example of Keralan architecture, showing the woodcarving characteristic of Kerala's art, as well as some fine murals and well-sculpted stone figures.

The palace comprises the royal dwelling quarters, the administrative areas, public spaces and a shrine. The interior is exquisite, especially the entrance hallway with its carved rosewood ceilings, and the Durbar hall that has floors finished with crushed shells, egg whites, coconuts and juices, and windows adorned with coloured mica.

About 63km (39 miles) southeast of Thiruvananthapuram, on the road to Kanyakumari. Tel: 04651 250 255. Open: Tue–Sun 9am–5pm. Nominal admission charge, camera and video charges.

Some of the exquisitely sculpted pillars at Padmanabhapuram Palace

Ponmudi

At an altitude of over 1,000m (3,280ft), Ponmudi is a lightly wooded hill resort. Banana, rubber, spice and tea plantations can be seen on the road up from Thiruvananthapuram, and the area is well known for its pleasant walks.
65km (40 miles) northeast of Thiruvananthapuram.

Varkala

The famous Krishna Temple here, **Janardhana Temple** (*Open: daily 5am–8pm*), was largely rebuilt in the 13th century, while the subsidiary shrines are said to be older than the temple itself. There are Saivite shrines outside the main complex, and on the cliff near the temple is the old palace of the Travancore Princely State, which has been converted into a government guesthouse (*Tel: 0470 260 2227*). Another attraction is **Papanasam Beach** at Varkala, which has been developed into a popular resort.
55km (34 miles) north of Thiruvananthapuram.

Veli Tourist Village

Veli has been developed as a tourist park along the shores of a lagoon stretching out to sea, and ending in a sandbar and a good beach with boating facilities. The landscaped gardens of the park contain fine sculptures by Kanayi Kunhiraman, known for their balance, harmony and erotic elements.
8km (5 miles) west of Thiruvananthapuram. Tel: 0471 250 0785. Open: 8am–7pm. Admission charge.

KOVALAM

Kovalam was the beach resort of the Maharajas of Travancore. Western tourists discovered its charms in the 1960s and 1970s when, like Goa, it became a hippy hang-out and started attracting backpackers and package holidaymakers. Today, Kovalam is one of Kerala's most popular tourist destinations and it rates among India's most visited beach resorts.

Aruvipuram

Literally 'the village of flowing waters', Aruvipuram on the **River Neyyar** attracts many pilgrims for ritual bathing, since the pilgrims believe that the river waters have healing properties. Pilgrims usually use the steps to wash their feet, but the waters are torrential so swimming is unsafe.
20km (12 miles) south of Thiruvananthapuram.

Beaches

Kovalam's main claim to fame is its four stretches of beach, separated from one another by rocky promontories or streams. Most of the tourists visit **Hawah Beach** (or Eve's Beach), and **Lighthouse Beach** near the striking red-and-white lighthouse on the headland. **Samudra Beach**, about 4km (2½ miles) north, is becoming an increasingly popular option. Some 8km (5 miles) south of Kovalam, beaches like **Chowara** and **Pullukudi** are gaining popularity as alternatives. Chowara is home to some of Kerala's best-known Ayurvedic centres.

Kanyakumari

A visit to Kanyakumari, the southern tip of India, undoubtedly forms the most popular day excursion from Kovalam. Kanyakumari means 'virgin maiden' and refers to Devi Karna who sought to become Shiva's consort by doing penance at the tip of India. When she was unsuccessful, Devi Karna proclaimed she would remain a virgin. The temple to Devi Karna is the site of one of the most important pilgrimages for Hindus. Devotees consider her to be the protector of the Indian shores. The **Vivekanand Memorial** is situated on a rock offshore from the mainland and gives spectacular views; it is dedicated to Swami Vivekanand who visited in 1892 as a devotee of the virgin goddess and stayed on to meditate. Inspired by his meditation, Swami Vivekanand spoke at the Parliament of Religions at Chicago and founded the Ramkrishna Mission at Chennai. The memorial built in 1970 integrates temple styles from different parts of India.
86km (53 miles) southeast of Thiruvananthapuram.

Neyyattinkara

The **Shri Krishna Temple** at this site (*www.sreekrishnaswamytemple.com. Opening hours variable*) dates from the 18th century; Raja Marthanda Varma is said to have stayed here.
The town is 20km (12 miles) from Thiruvananthapuram on National Highway 47. There is a holy bathing

The coast at Kovalam – an earthly paradise

site on the Neyyar River about 4km (2½ miles) from the town.

Padmanabhapuram
See pp30–31.

Suchindram
Unusually, the temple at Suchindram is shared by the trinity of Vishnu, Brahma and Shiva. The temple has an ornately decorated towering *gopuram* (temple gatehouse), and to the north is an enormous tank with a shelter in the middle. Founded during the Pandiyan reign, which reached its zenith in the 12th and 13th centuries and expanded under the Nayakas of Thirumalai in the 17th century, the temple became part of the Travancore Princely State and houses treasures from different kingdoms. Among the interesting sculptures are those depicting Shiva, his consort and sons, as well as a towering Hanuman statue inside.
14km (9 miles) from Kanyakumari. Open: daily 3am–1pm, 4–8pm. Usually open to non-Hindus. Sunset ceremonies on Friday.

Vizhinjam
This was the capital of the Ay rulers who were a dominant force in Travancore's history. Once controlled by the Pandiyans in the 7th century, the Ay rulers rose to prominence 200 years later. Now largely a fishing village, Vizhinjam has an 8th-century shrine with figures cut into the rock.
3km (2 miles) from Kovalam.

The home of Ayurveda

Ayurveda probably started in the Himalayas in about the 6th century BC, and is a type of herbal medicine which is used in most parts of India. It is associated with Kerala on account of the many colleges and hospitals, such as the one at Kottakal, and the many Ayurvedic resorts that have recently become established in the state. The word Ayurveda is derived from the Sanskrit words for 'wisdom', or 'science', or 'life', and the philosophy is based on a holistic understanding of the human body, mind and spirit; illness affects both the body and the mind, and these should therefore not be treated separately. Physical and emotional health can be maintained by balancing energies, and diagnosis is based on the philosophy that illness is the result of a loss of balance of *doshas*, a combination of elements that comprise the human body, making use of the 107 *marmas* or sensitive points. Ayurvedic physicians prescribe traditional healing techniques such as purification, diet, herbal medicine, massage, meditation and yoga.

Ayurveda was discouraged by the British Raj, but after India became

Dhara – an Ayurvedic treatment involving a flow of herbal oil onto the patient's forehead

independent in 1947, it was promoted by the government as an important form of medicine.

For most visitors to Kerala, the most enjoyable and relaxing Ayurvedic treatment is a massage, which is also the first cleansing therapy offered to most patients as a form of pre-detoxification. The massage oils have properties that help to heal and protect the skin; the therapist uses gentle, circular movements – with the degree of pressure depending on the patient's condition – covering the head and the body, and the massage is followed by a steam bath. Some resorts also offer synchronised massages by two or more therapists, as well as Chavatti-Uzhichil, which is done by foot instead of by hand, for rejuvenation, muscle toning, weight loss and improved circulation.

The Ayurvedic programmes offered by most hotels and resorts are *Rasayana Chikitsa* (rejuvenation therapy), *Kayakalpa Chikitsa* (body immunisation and longevity therapy), *Sveda Karma* (involving body cleansing by inducing perspiration as part of pre-detoxification) and *Panchakarma* (for overall wellbeing). Many resorts provide programmes for patients suffering from rheumatic and arthritic problems, backaches and chronic ailments. Meditation, yoga and stress-relief programmes are also popular.

The treatments on offer at Ayurvedic resorts include the following:

Dhara: In Sirodhara, a thin flow of herbal oil, from a pot with a hole suspended over the patient's head, is directed to a spot on the forehead near the eyebrows and then stroked down the hair by the therapist and allowed to permeate the skin. The oil may be massaged into the scalp if prescribed by the physician. Other forms of *dhara* involve the pouring of buttermilk, fermented yoghurt-based fluids or medicated milk over the forehead or body.

Karnapoornam: Ear treatment.

Marma Kizhi: Massage with herbal powder-filled cloth bags.

Nasyam or Nasya Karma: Nasal therapy, which involves inhaling medicated vapours.

Pizhichil: A herbal compress.

Sirolepam: Application of herbal pastes chosen for the patient.

Snehapanam: Administers ghee internally for those with osteoarthritis, leukaemia and other ailments.

Sveda: Induces perspiration by application of herbal bundles, along with medicated steam baths or herbal tub baths.

Tharpanam and Ajanam: Eye treatments.

Udvarthanam: Herbal powder massage.

Urovasti: Administration of oil to the chest.

KOLLAM
Kollam town

Surrounded by coconut palm and cashew plantations, the market town of Kollam, or Quilon, is situated on the edge of Ashtamudi Lake. As one of the gateways to the waterways of Kerala, Kollam was an important trading city coveted by colonial powers, and some of its old, red-tiled wooden houses still line the narrow, winding streets.

Known to Marco Polo as Koilum, it traded with Europe, the Middle East and China, and evidence of Chinese connections still survives in its ceramics and in the style of fishing nets lining the backwaters.

In the 9th century, Kollam was the capital of the Venadu Dynasty; today it is known as a convenient staging post for boat trips on the backwaters.
Kollam is 61km (38 miles) northwest of Thiruvananthapuram, 119km (74 miles) from Kochi and 280km (174 miles) from Kozhikode, with good road and rail connections.

Ashtamudi Lake

Literally 'seven creeks', Ashtamudi Lake extends north from Kollam. It is an attractive lake with palm-fringed banks and promontories extending into the water, where dugouts carry coir, copra (coconut kernel), cashew and fish. Boat tours on the canals of Ashtamudi provide a good way of experiencing village life, coir weaving, copra drying, fish and shrimp farming, matchstick making and agriculture. Plans are afoot to restore the lake, limiting the effects of pollution and boosting local industry and ecotourism.
5km (3 miles) northwest of central Kollam. Boats leave from the KSRTC bus stand at the south end of the lake.

Mukkada Bazaar

The series of parallel streets that make up the bazaar are teeming with spice warehouses, metal merchants and rope makers plying their trade. The best time to go is late afternoon.
South of Main Road.

Shrine of Our Lady of Velankanni

One of the landmark buildings of Kollam, this is an unusual-looking Christian shrine, in the shape of a pyramid and topped by a golden Madonna.
Situated near Alappuzha Road.

KETTUVALAMS

Kettuvalams are strong and sturdy boats capable of carrying heavy loads. Often called rice boats, the *Kettuvalams* are used for cargo and as a means of transport, and they are made from wooden planks tied together with coir, with a thatched roof to protect people and cargo from the rain. In deep water the boatman uses an oar to propel the boat along, but in shallower water he uses a long bamboo pole.

The *Kettuvalam* declined in importance when road transport began to make most of the waterways redundant, but today many of them have been remodelled as passenger boats and houseboats (*see p130*).

Kollam environs

Kayyamkulam

Some 33km (21 miles) north of
Kollam, Alamakadavu on the outskirts
of Kayyamkulam is a centre for the
construction of Kerala's rice boats,
called *Kettuvalams* (*see opposite*).

Krishnapuram Palace

Raja Marthanda Varma built this
palace near Kayyamkulam in the
18th century, probably expanding
older royal residences that existed here.
Renovated in 1999, the two-storey
palace is a good example of Keralan
architecture, with gabled roofs and
woodcarvings, and it still has its
original bathing tank inside. The palace
contains the mural of *Gajendra
Moksha*, one of the largest wall
paintings in Kerala, depicting the
Bhagwad story of the deliverance of the
elephant chief by Lord Vishnu.

Now a museum, the palace exhibits
sculptures and paintings from various
archaeological sites and copies
of murals from Mattancherry Palace,
as well as some from other temples
and churches. One of the prized
exhibits is a palanquin (a covered seat
enclosed by curtains and carried on
men's shoulders) used by the married
women of the royal family, and an
ancient Buddha statue stands in the
landscaped garden.
*39km (24 miles) north of Kollam.
Tel: 0479 244 1133. Open: Tue–Sun
10am–1pm & 2–5pm.
Small admission charge.*

Fishing boats on the beach near Kollam

Valliakvu

Also called Amritapuri, Valliakvu is
home to the ashram of Mata
Amritanandamayi (*Tel: 0476 289 7578.
www.amritapuri.org. Programme: daily
from 5am. Public darshan Wed, Thur,
Sat & Sun 10am*), whose Mission Trust
supports a variety of projects such as
orphanages and hospitals.
12km (7 miles) south of Kayyamkulam.

ALAPPUZHA
Alappuzha town

Alappuzha, or Alleppey, is a market town clustered along a network of canals. The waterways are still in use and service the coir industry that has thrived here since the 19th century. Another important industry here is cashew processing, and some of the old factories and warehouses still stand.
Alappuzha is 130km (81 miles) northwest of Thiruvananthapuram, 56km (35 miles) south of Kochi and 205km (127 miles) south of Kozhikode, with good road and rail connections.

Temples

The **Mullakal Devi Temple** (*Muhakal Road, just south of junction with Cullan Road*) is among several that participate in a festival every December, which is celebrated with music, dance, rituals and processions. Alappuzha also has a modern **Jain Shwemtambar Temple**, built next to the older Jain shrine.
Just north of South Canal, towards the beach. Open: daily 6–8am & 4.30–8pm.

Alappuzha environs
Ambalapuzha
Sree Krishna Ananda Temple
(*Opening hours variable*) at Ambalapuzha is one of the most important temples of the erstwhile Travancore State. Designed in typical Keralan style, with gabled roofs and carved wooden façades, it is set beside a sacred tank. Milk rice is offered at the temple and is considered as the gift of a Brahmin to the poor.
About 14km (9 miles) south of the town centre.

Aranmula

Aranmula is well known as the centre of bell-metal handicrafts, and especially for its famous mirrors. It has a **Parthasarathy Temple** (*Open: daily 4.30–11.30am or noon & 5 or 5.30–8.30pm*) to Lord Krishna as the charioteer for Arjuna, a central figure in the Hindu epic *Mahabharata*. There is also a boat race, with devotees believing that Krishna is in every boat.
10km (6 miles) east of Chengannur.

Traversing the backwaters of Alappuzha

Arthunkal

The **St Sebastian Church** (*Tel: 0478 257 2374. www.arthunkalchurch.org. Open: 8am–8pm. Free admission*) at Arthunkal was built in 1591 and is well known for the procession that carries the saint's statue to the beach in January. *About 25km (16 miles) north of the town centre via Mararikulam.*

Haripad

Haripad has one of Kerala's most important Subramanya Temples, which houses an idol of the four-armed deity which devotees believe was found in the river.
16km (10 miles) south of Alappuzha on National Highway 47 leading to Kollam. Haripad is one of the major centres for boat races and festivals in August and December.

Mannarasala

The **Nagaraja Temple** here (*Tel: 0479 241 3214. www.mannarasala.org. Opening hours variable*) is one of the most important of the many temples located in the 'snake groves' of Kerala. The surrounding woodlands have several statues of snake gods and hooded cobras among the trees and along the paths leading to the temple dedicated to the Snake King, Nagaraja. Childless women visit the shrine to pray for a child, and, if they have one, they return to donate the equivalent weight of the baby in grain to the temple.

The temple is best known for its association with the *Mahabharata* which mentions the fleeing of snakes to a place devotees believe is Mannarasala. Unusually, the temple has a priestess as the local Namboodri Brahmin women are said to have planted sacred groves for the snakes. In typical Keralan architectural style, the temple's main shrine is dedicated to Nagaraja, the serpent king, and his consort.

Thousands of Hindus attend the temple's annual festival in September or October, when its idols are carried through the woods, and offerings of milk, rice and turmeric are made. *About 32km (20 miles) south of Alappuzha.*

Mararikulam

The fishing hamlet of Mararikulam provides access to the excellent **Marari Beach**, which is a popular resort. *15km (9 miles) north of Alappuzha.*

BOAT RACES

On the second Saturday of August, the Nehru Boat Race at Alappuzha is one of Kerala's most famous regattas, and thousands come to watch the race on Vembanad Lake. Behind the stern of each snake boat, shaped like the hood of a cobra, a hundred or so rowers power their way across the waters, shouting and singing enthusiastically. The rowers are supported by helmsmen and women, who do the steering, and cheered by singers and spectators from their village. The crowd avidly watches a tradition that harks back to the time when the snake boats transported troops to battle.

Boat races are also a feature of the Onam celebrations elsewhere in Kerala. At Payipad near Haripad, the boat races are said to be in honour of the finding of the idol of Subhramanya at Haripad, while at Aranmula the boats carry effigies of Lord Krishna.

The backwaters of paradise

A unique aspect of Kerala's geography is its backwaters, a network of rivers, streams, lagoons, lakes, canals and tanks that runs along most of its coastline. The best-known stretch is from Kollam to Kochi, the northern section of which is called Kuttinad. The backwaters have few outlets to the sea and the lagoons depend on rivers for their water. In the monsoon season, seawater enters parts of the inland lagoons and canals: this combination of saline and fresh water is essential to the aquatic life of the backwaters, including the coveted *karimeen* fish.

Touring the backwaters is one of the highlights of a visit to Kerala.

Waterfront activities like coir-making, rice-growing, toddy-tapping and fishing can be seen along the banks, and traditional dugouts ply the waterways. The banks are green with coconut palms and groves of mango, papaya, jackfruit and other trees, and tapioca is among the crops grown here. Travelling the backwaters also gives a glimpse of village life; entire settlements are located on strips of land separating the waterways, and the houses have poultry, cattle, pigs and ducks, and even vegetable gardens. Prawns and fish are farmed, sand is dredged for construction, and shells are collected for the production of lime. The boats pass canals where

A boatman cruising along the backwaters

Chinese fishing nets are a distinctive feature of the backwaters

coconuts, coir, cashews and food are loaded onto dugouts.

The most popular backwater trip is the journey from Kollam to Alappuzha, or vice versa, which takes about eight hours, usually departing at 10.30am, with halts along the way, to the coir village of Thrikkunnapuzha, to islands such as Lekshmithuruthy, and to popular spots such as the ashram at Amritapuri. Shorter trips are also available from Kollam, Alappuzha and Kochi, and from the northern backwaters near Kozhikode and Bekal. Some cruises, such as those from Alappuzha and Kottayam, include toddy tasting in their itinerary.

Apart from tours, passenger boats and public ferries, it is also possible to hire motorboats and speedboats for travelling around the backwaters.

Hotels and resorts at Kottayam, Kumarakom, Alappuzha and Kollam also organise backwater cruises and short boat trips. The best, but more expensive, option is to charter a houseboat.

TROUBLED WATERS

Although travellers see a somewhat idyllic side of life on Kerala's backwaters, these areas are not free of environmental problems. Reclaimed land for agriculture has reduced the surface-water area, and almost all the mangrove vegetation has been destroyed. The construction of barriers across Vembanad Lake is one of the many changes that has affected the ecology, along with increased population density and pollution. Despite initiatives from the Ministry of the Environment, and in particular the National Mangrove Committee, and calls to action from the National Institute of Oceanography, the mangroves continue to deteriorate, with Kerala's the worst hit in the country.

KOTTAYAM
Kottayam city

Kottayam is sandwiched between the hills to the east and the backwaters to the west, with fertile lands on the outskirts producing rubber and other cash crops. The Christian population of Kerala followed the Syrian Orthodox Church, but after attempts by the Portuguese to Latinise the Church, the Syrian Christians took an oath stating that the Portuguese priests were not their leaders.

The Syrian Church became an autonomous body without links to Rome. Many Syrian Christians subsequently rejoined the Roman Church after a visit by the Pope, but one group formed the Jacobite Syrian Christian Church. After independence, most of the churches reunited, and Kottayam's history of Syrian Christian settlement is reflected in its churches.

Kottayam is also known for its high literacy rate, and it publishes some of the most read Malayalam newspapers. Many well-known Malayalam writers hail from Kottayam, and a cooperative was established here in 1945.

Cheria Palli (St Mary's Church)

The elegant St Mary's Church, called Cheria Palli, is some 450 years old and is situated on top of a hill. Its interior displays some beautiful murals on the walls and ceiling, and above the altar.
2km (1¼ miles) north of the town centre. Tel: 0481 256 6744. www.cheriapally.com. Open: 8am–6pm. Free admission.

Thirunakkara Shiva Temple

This temple is in typical Keralan style, with an interesting *Kootiattum*, the traditional temple theatre for religious dance drama.
Temple Road (at the junction with Azad Lane), in the centre of town. Usually open: daily 5am–noon & 5–8pm.

Valiya Palli

This church was built in the 16th century and is famous for its Persian Cross with a Pahlavi inscription next to the altar. Another cross has a Syriac liturgy. There is also an unusual portrayal of St George slaying a dragon. The guest book has comments dating from 1899, and among its entries is one by an Ethiopian emperor.
2km (1¼ miles) north of the town centre. Tel: 0481 256 3324. www.kottayamvaliyapally.com. Opening hours variable. Free admission.

Kottayam environs
Chengannur

Chengannur has three interesting temples, all worth a visit – a Mahadev Temple with a theatre on an old plinth; a Bhagwati Temple, which is said to bring good fortune to devotees; and a small 18th-century Narasimha Temple.
About 30km (19 miles) south of Kottayam, 1km (²⁄₃ mile) off the highway to Thiruvananthapuram.

Ettumanoor

See p44.

Kaviyur

Kaviyur has one of Kerala's best-preserved caves, dating from the 8th century and notable for its carved reliefs. It also houses a pillared hall, a shrine and a *linga* (a phallic image of the god Shiva).

5km (3 miles) from Thiruvalla on the rail route to Thiruvananthapuram, east of the main road.

Kumarakom

With its **bird sanctuary** (*Tel: 0481 252 5864. Open: daily 6am–5.30pm. Admission charge*), backwater villages and islands, Kumarakom has seen the development of tourist resorts around it. Here you can arrange boat trips to see the birdlife, which is at its best from November to February when migrants from the north make it their winter home (*see p131*). This is also a good spot to experience traditional farming life and village activities.

About 16km (10 miles) north of Kottayam. Buses leave from the KSRTC bus stand in Kottayam for Kumarakom every 15 minutes.

St John's Cathedral

Designed by Laurie Baker, this Syrian Christian church is built in Keralan architectural style with a tiled roof, timber ceiling and a circular interior that has no visible support. It was built to mark the anniversary of the martyrdom of St Thomas.

On the road to Thiruvalla from Kottayam. Tel: 0469 260 4933.

Thiruvalla

Thiruvalla is home to the **Shri Vallabh Temple**, which is noted for its night-time Kathakali performances.

South of Kottayam on the road and rail route to Thiruvananthapuram. Temple open: daily 4.30–11.30am & 5–8pm. Kathakali performances 10pm–1am.

The highly adorned altar of a Syrian Orthodox church in Kottayam

Tour: North of Kottayam

The road north from Kottayam to Kochi criss-crosses rivers and backwaters, and two of Kerala's most important temples can be seen on this route.

From Kottayam to Vaikom, via the diversion to Palai, is 67km (42 miles). Allow half a day.

Drive 12km (8 miles) north from Kottayam towards Kochi. The Shiva temple of Ettumanoor is on the right-hand side, with parking available on the road heading east to Palai.

1 Ettumanoor

The **Mahadev Temple** (*Open: daily 4am–12.30pm & 5–8pm*) at Ettumanoor is one of the wealthiest in Kerala. Built in the typical Keralan style in the 16th century, the temple is noted for its woodcarvings. Beautiful murals on the *gopuram* (gatehouse) depict Vishnu in the form of Padmanabha reclining on a serpent, and Shiva as Natraj crushing evil, as well as the lives of Rama and Krishna, and Shaivite figures in the halls. The murals are similar in style to those in the Mattancherry Palace of Kochi (*see pp52–3*). The main shrine is circular, with a conical, copper-clad interior ceiling, enclosing a square sanctuary. There is a large festival here in February or March, when gold elephant statues are put on display.
A hilly road travels east from Ettumanoor to Palai, passing rubber plantations on the way.

2 Palai

Palai, or Pala, on the Meenachil River, is the gateway to the southern ranges of the Western Ghats. It is also an important hub for Roman Catholic Syrian Christians in India and has several impressive churches, one of which, **St Mary's Church of Bharananganam** (*Tel: 0482 223 7144. www.stmarybharananganam.com.*

THE PILGRIMAGE TO SABARIMALA

Kottayam lies on the route of the famous pilgrimage to the Ayyapa Temple of Sabarimala from Thiruvananthapuram. After Kottayam comes Erumeli where thousands of pilgrims, dressed in black, worship at a mosque dedicated to Varr. From Erumeli, the 60km (38-mile) track has to be covered on foot, passing Chalakayam and Pampa, with stops for ceremonies at a number of pilgrim sites en route. Pilgrims have to face a steep, two-hour jungle walk to the shrine, which is 914m (2,999ft) above sea level. Eighteen golden steps symbolise various sins, and when ascending the steps, pilgrims take an oath to give up these sins.

Those who do not want to make the entire pilgrimage can take a bus to Chalakayam and then walk 8km (5 miles) to Sabarimala.

Opening hours variable), is believed to date from the 11th century. Palai also boasts the Shrine of Kurishupalli as well as a number of old Syrian Christian houses on the rubber plantations. *Retrace your tracks from Palai to Ettumanoor, and then turn north on the SH15 to Kochi. At Kuruppanthara, turn left, then left again on to the SH42 at Kallara. Turn right to Vaikom at the junction with the SH40.*

3 Vaikom

Vaikom (*www.vaikomtemple.org. Open: daily 3.30am–noon & 5–8.30pm*) is one of the holiest Shiva temples in Kerala and is enshrined in myth. The temple's present structure probably dates from the 16th century and its murals from the 18th century. These depict Shiva, Parvati and Ganesha, Vishnu with his consort, among other figures.

In 1925, the temple was one of the first to allow untouchables to visit the main sanctuary. By 1928, the Maharaja of Travancore had opened temples to Hindus of all castes throughout his princely state.

The temple has a 12-day festival in November and December, with a particularly auspicious last night. Deities from nearby temples are brought here throughout the festival. *From Vaikom you can drive back to Kottayam or continue on the road to Kochi.*

Kerala's architecture

Although centuries of maritime contact and colonisation mean that Kerala's architecture has absorbed regional and international influences, it nevertheless retains a distinctive identity. Its distinguishing features include pagoda shapes, steeply pitched sloping roofs with gables and eaves, columned galleries and open courtyards. The main building materials are grass, clay and stone, and roofs are made of timber, terracotta tiles and thatch. Flooring is usually made from clay tiles.

In some parts of Kerala, houses are made from intricately interlocked wooden grids and panels, eschewing the use of a single nail or adhesives. The builders of Kerala follow directions for the correct construction of houses given by architectural treatises such as the *Vastu Shastra*, *Vastuvidya*, *Manushyalaya Chandrika*, *Vastupurusha Mandala* and the *Silparatna of Sri Kumara*: these provide instructions on the importance of location, the use of natural resources, and the various techniques for providing the best air-flow, light and water storage.

Churches

Kerala's churches are generally European in style, with an elaborately decorated backdrop to the altar. Usually cruciform or rectangular, they have large halls for the congregation. Unlike temples, which are generally located near water sources for ritual bathing, most of the churches of Kerala have hilltop locations.

Mosques

The early mosques of Kerala were built in the distinctive regional style, and good examples can be found in Kozhikode dating from the 16th century. In more recent times, the mosques have adopted the Middle-Eastern model.

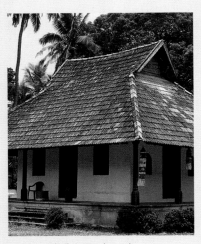

A museum built in Keralan style, Thiruvananthapuram

Nallukettu

The *Nallukettu*, or four-winged courtyard house, is probably the most beautiful garden dwelling in India and is certainly one of the country's finest examples of wooden architecture. It is centred around a sunken courtyard, which is designed to collect water, and also to ventilate the house with columned verandahs on all sides and galleries leading to the four blocks of the house. Guests are received in a reception room near the entrance and in a number of large halls which are used for entertainment. Louvred (dome-shaped) wooden ventilators and adjustable roofs ensure adequate air-flow and light, and the layout is flexible to accommodate the addition of more rooms.

The *Ettukettu* is an extended version of the *Nallukettu*, with eight blocks enclosing the courtyard. These mansions are large, with gardens, sheds, bathing ponds, wells and granaries. The *Illam* of the Namboodri Brahmins is similar to a *Nallukettu*, but is usually more compact.

Temples

Kerala's temples are rarely taller than the trees that surround them. Entered through a gatehouse, or *gopuram*, the temple has steeply pitched roofs and the interior ceiling is usually covered with copper sheaths.

The temple clusters around the main sanctum with subsidiary shrines and an entrance hall, which is called a *mandapam*. The upper parts of the sanctuary interiors are intricately decorated with carvings or paintings to denote the importance of the *garbhagriha*, home of the deity. Most temples have a theatre called the *Koothambalam*.

A traditional Keralan lock with intricate detail

KOCHI (COCHIN)
Kochi city

Cosmopolitan and laid-back, Kochi is one of Southern India's most charming cities. Its lively restaurant and cultural scenes are a world away from the rudimentary tourist infrastructure elsewhere in the region, making the town a rewarding stop-off on any journey through Kerala.

Much of its relaxed vibe comes from the water that permeates the city. A natural harbour – the result of Malabar mud banks – separates the towns of Kochi and Ernakulam, which together make up the conurbation that was known in the British era as Cochin. Consequently, getting around town often requires the use of a bridge or ferry, which, while it doesn't make for the quickest journeys, can be very pleasant for the leisure traveller. The watery surroundings also have the effect of making the city feel very clean by Indian standards.

Its aquatic location made Kochi the ideal gateway to India for seafaring foreigners, who have been using it as such for more than five centuries. The Chinese, Portuguese, Dutch, Mysoreans and British all came and went, and this cultural mélange is evident in the architecture and open outlook of the city. There is also Jew Town, one of Kochi's top tourist districts, to add to the mix.

That area, along with Mattancherry and Fort Cochin, lies to the west of Vembanad Lake, part of a series of islets and peninsulas that boast most of the tourist attractions. East of the water on the mainland is Ernakulam, the hub of the city.

Kochi is 220km (137 miles) north of Thiruvananthapuram and has an airport, good rail connections to most cities in India and road access to other parts of Kerala. The Government of India tourist office is at Willingdon Island, the Kerala Tourism Development Corporation is on Shanmugham Road and the District Tourism Promotion Office is at the Old Collectorate Building, Park Avenue (Tel: 0484 236 7334).

Art galleries

The local art scene has flourished in Kochi, and art lovers have plenty of venues from which to choose.

Chitram Art Gallery, *MG Road, Ravipuram. Tel: 0484 309 6812. Open: daily 9.30am–8pm. Free admission.*

Dravidian Art and Performance Gallery, *Bazaar Road, south of customs jetty. Tel: 0484 309 6812. Open: daily 9am–5pm. Free admission.*

Kashi Art Gallery, *Burgher Street. Tel: 0484 221 5769. www.kashiartgallery.com. Open: daily 10am–12.30pm, 2–6pm. Free admission.*

Bolgatty Island

The palatial mansion at Bolgatty was built in 1744 when the Dutch controlled Kochi and later became a British residency. With its acres of lawns and gardens, this old residency has been converted into a resort. *www.bolgattyislandresortkochi.com*

Santa Cruz Basilica

This Roman Catholic church at Fort Kochi was built in the 16th century but had to be rebuilt in the 1800s. Notable features include the woodcarvings and murals inside. In 1984, Pope John Paul II raised the church to the status of Basilica. *Near St Francis Church. Open: daily 9am–1pm & 3–5pm. English Mass Sat 6pm & Sun 4.30pm.*

St Francis Church

Originally dedicated to Saint Anthony, this is reputedly India's first European-built church and one of the oldest churches in Southern India. Built of wood by Portuguese friars in 1503, the church was rebuilt in stone later in the same century. The oldest inscriptions found in the church are dated to 1562. Vasco da Gama was buried here in 1524, until, 14 years later, his remains were shipped to Lisbon.

Over the years the church has experienced a number of conversions and it is now used by the Church of South India. The building is impressive and an unusual feature is its rope-operated *punkah* (fan). *Mon–Fri 9.30am–1pm & 2.30–5pm, Sat 2.30–5pm. Free admission.*

Temples

Ernakulathappan Temple in Ernakulam is known for its association with the legend of Nagarishi, who was

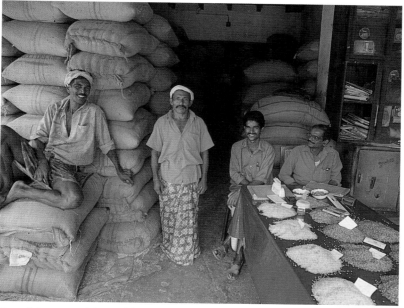

Rice outlets are essential to trade in Kochi

given a snake's head as a curse for killing a snake. This legend is celebrated in January with ceremonies and cultural events.

Sixteen kilometres (10 miles) northwest from Ernakulam is the **Chottanikkara Temple**, which is a popular pilgrimage site. The main deity is worshipped as Sarasvati in the morning, Bhagwati in the afternoon and Durga in the evening, and the temple is also the site of a nine-day festival in February and March.
Ernakulathappan Temple, Durbar Hall Road (at roundabout with Foreshaw Road), Ernakulam. Open: daily 3.30–11am & 4–8pm. Chottanikkara Temple is 16km (10 miles) northwest of Ernakulam, from where there are regular buses. Tel: 0484 271 1032. www.chottanikkarabhagavathy.org. Open: 4am–12.30pm & 4–9pm. Admission for Hindus only.

Vypeen Island
Vypeen Island is home to the **Pallipuram Fort** (*Open: Thur dawn–dusk*). It was built by the Portuguese in the 16th century and taken by the Dutch in 1663. The island also has a lighthouse, and its beaches are becoming increasingly popular with holidaymakers. *Vypeen Island lies 450m (¼ mile) from Fort Cochin ferry jetty.*

Kochi environs
Chennamangalam
Once the seat of the Palayathachan, hereditary ministers of Kochi Princely

State, Chennamangalam has a 17th-century palace presented to it by the Dutch. The palace is now part of a trust that looks after 60 or so temples in and around the village.

The village also has interesting historical associations with the Jews, who built their oldest synagogue here (now largely in ruins), as well as with the Jesuit Christians and the Muslims. The 16th-century mosque still stands, but the Jesuit seminary was destroyed by Tipu Sultan.

Kodungallur, near Chennamangalam, is believed to be the port of Muziris mentioned by Pliny, and is also the place where St Thomas is said to have landed, bringing Christianity to Kerala. Malik Ibn Dinar, who first brought Islam to India, built Kerala's first mosque, **Cheraman** (*Tel: 0480 280 3170. www.cheramanmosque.com*), at Kodungallur. The mosque that now stands here probably dates from the 18th century.
42km (26 miles) north of Ernakulam.

CHINESE FISHING NETS
Chinese fishing nets were probably introduced when Kerala traded with the Chinese court. The nets are framed with wood and strung along poles that can be 3m (10ft) long, tied to suspended boulders. The boulders help keep the net down when it is dipped into the water at high tide. Four or five men pull the net out of the water using a rope with a pulley system and rocks at the other end to balance the weight. The nets bring in large catches, and a good place to see them in action is at Kochi.

Fishermen using traditional Chinese nets can often be seen at Kochi

Museum of Kerala History

This museum makes good use of paintings, sculptures, sound-and-light effects and audiovisual aids to depict the history of Kerala from the Neolithic period through the arrival of colonial forces to modern times.

Edapally, 10km (6 miles) north of Ernakulam towards Thrissur. www.artandkeralahistory.org. Open: 10am–noon & 2–4pm.

Tripunithura

Tripunithura has the **Hill Palace Museum,** with its collection of coins, manuscripts, scriptures and princely relics of Kochi and Travancore.

Chottanikkara Road, 12km (8 miles) southeast of Ernakulam. Tel: 0480 278 1113. Open: Tue–Sun 9am–4.30pm (may close for lunch 12.30–2pm). Small admission charge.

Walk: Mattancherry

This walk through Mattancherry, near Fort Kochi, offers an opportunity to see Kochi Synagogue, the royal palace and the Jew Town Market, a spice trade centre. Though the latter will involve the hard sell, the atmosphere and charm of the streets make it worth putting up with the repeated sales pitches.

Allow 4 hours, including time for shopping.

Start at the Mattancherry Palace, which has good road and ferry access to the rest of Kochi.

1 Mattancherry Palace

Also called the Dutch Palace, this palace was actually built by the Portuguese in the 16th century and gifted to their ally, the ruler of Kochi, who gave them trading rights. The palace was practically rebuilt after the Dutch took over Kochi in 1663. Built on two floors around a quadrangle, it incorporates European influences into the traditional *Nallukettu* plan (*see p47*). It has a Bhagvati Temple in the central courtyard and Shiva and Vishnu temples to the south.

The palace is renowned for its marvellous murals from the 16th and 17th centuries depicting the entire *Ramayana* and scenes from the *Mahabharata*. The Central Hall was used for coronation ceremonies and has an interesting display of dresses, turbans and palanquins.

JEWRY OF KOCHI

In Jew Town you are likely to hear stories about Jews who arrived here in King Solomon's ships about the 9th century BC, those who arrived in Kerala fleeing Babylon in the 6th century BC, those who arrived from Assyria in search of refuge, as well as those who migrated to Kerala after the destruction of Jerusalem in the 1st century AD and the 10,000 Jews who fled from Palestine in the 2nd century and were allowed to settle at Muziris (probably Kodungallur).

Ideal go-betweens for the local Malayalam population and overseas traders, Jews became one of Kerala's most influential communities. Raja Bhaskara Ravi Varma, who ruled in the 10th and 11th centuries, granted the Jewish community the village of Anjuvaddam and its surrounding land. By the 16th century the Arabs and Portuguese had all but destroyed the Jewish community in Kerala, who then moved to Kochi and were granted protection, land and titles. Their population was augmented by those fleeing persecution in Europe. The Jewish population dwindled with the mass migration to Israel in the 20th century, and today only a few Jewish families live in Kochi.

Tel: 0484 222 6085. Open: Sat–Thur
10am–5pm. Admission charge.
*From the main gate of the Mattancherry
Palace, head right for the synagogue.*

2 Kochi Synagogue

Also called the Mattancherry Pardesi
Synagogue, this was founded in 1568
and rebuilt by the Dutch in 1664, two
years after the Portuguese destroyed
the building. A wealthy Jewish
merchant, Ezekial Rahabi, donated the
clock tower in the 18th century.
Notable features include Cantonese
willow-pattern tiles, Belgian
chandeliers, interlocking pews, gilt
columns, ornate brass pulpit and a slab
from the 14th-century Kochangadi
Synagogue that is now in ruins.

Open: Sun–Thur 10am–noon & 3–5pm.
Admission charge.
*Head south from the synagogue for the
pepper exchange, established to fuel
foreign investment in the spice trade.
The pepper exchange marks the start of
the Jew Town Market.*

3 Jew Town Market

The market has developed into a
bazaar for antiques, curios, handicrafts
and tourist souvenirs, with shops
selling anything from Kathakali
masks, jewel boxes and trinkets to
ornate bullock carts.
*From Jew Town retrace your steps along
the waterfront to return to Mattancherry
Palace or to catch a ferry (from the Jetty)
to Ernakulam or Kochi.*

Kerala

THRISSUR
Thrissur city

Thrissur is an abbreviation of Thiru, Shiva and Perur, meaning 'the city named after Lord Shiva', and for centuries it has been an important religious and cultural centre. Widely regarded as Kerala's cultural capital, Thrissur District is famous for its temples, churches, arts colleges and training schools for southern Indian performing arts.

Located at the western end of the Palakkad (or Palghat) Gap, Thrissur formed a vital link between the coast and the interior of the peninsula. The Rajas of Central Kerala reigned from here before moving their capital to Kochi. Thrissur fell to the Zamorin of Malabar, then Sultan Hyder Ali, and eventually to the European colonial powers.
Thrissur has good road and rail connections to Thiruvananthapuram, Kozhikode and Kochi. The tourist information offices are at the Government Guest House and near the Town Hall.

Our Lady of Lourdes Cathedral

This cathedral has an impressive Indo-European façade with soaring pink spires. The interior of the cathedral is notable for its attractive underground shrine.
About 1km (²/₃ mile) out of the town centre towards Peechi. Tel: 0487 233 3995. www.lourdescathedralthrissur.com. Open: daily 6.30am–6.30pm. Free admission.

Vadakkunnathan Temple

Traditionally this temple on a hillock is regarded as the centre of Thrissur, with roads radiating on all sides. The temple is an excellent example of Kerala's architecture, with fine woodcarvings decorating the roof and façade. Predominantly a Shiva temple, it also has shrines to other deities. The main sanctuaries are dedicated to Shiva as Vadakkunnathan, and to Sankara Narayan, with a Ganesh shrine between them. The interior has beautiful murals near the main shrines. Entry is for Hindus only, but visitors are usually allowed on special days, including the famous Pooram Festival.
Tel: 0487 242 6040. Open: daily 4.30–11.30am & 5–8.30pm.

Thrissur environs
Angamali

This is an important Syrian Christian centre and it was once home to one of the most important bishoprics in Kerala. Nearby, at Akaparambhu, the church of Mar Sabore and Afroth (*opening hours variable*) was founded in the 9th century, although the present structure dates from after the 16th century and shows some Portuguese influences. It is particularly noted for its murals narrating stories from the Bible.
32km (20 miles) south of Thrissur on National Highway 47 to Ernakulam.

Guruvayoor

Guruvayoor, on the coast 16km (10 miles) northwest of Thrissur, is an important religious centre for the worship of the infant Krishna. According to one of the legends associated with the temple, the site was selected by Guru, preceptor of the gods, and Vayu, lord of the winds, when they met Lord Shiva and Parvati with Parashurama, creator of Kerala, at the tank of Guruvayoor. The tank has a statue of Krishna playing the flute. The temple has carved columns, a tall gold flagpost, called the *dhvajastambha*, a lamp tower, some murals and the image of a four-armed Krishna with a conch, a discus, a mace and a lotus.

The 16th-century poet Narayana Bhattatiri wrote the famous Hindu text *Narayaneeyam* (inspired by the Bhagwad) at Guruvayoor. A sufferer of rheumatic illness, he was cured during his visit to Guruvayoor, and since then the temple is regularly visited by people with rheumatism seeking recovery through the blessings of the infant Krishna. The temple is also a popular location for marriage ceremonies.

Our Lady of Lourdes Metropolitan Cathedral, Thrissur

Elephants on parade at the Pooram Festival in Thrissur (*see p19*)

The temple elephants are housed at the Punnathur Kotha, an old fortified complex. This is a good place to see the elephants being bathed by the *mahouts* (drivers), but visitors must be careful, as the animals can be dangerous, especially the males during the breeding season. Wild elephants are brought here to be tamed for the temple festivals.
Tel: 0487 255 6335.
devaswom.guruvayur@gmail.com.
Open: daily 3am–12.30pm &
4.30–9.15pm. Opening times may vary. Non-Hindus are not permitted to enter. Regular buses from Thrissur to the bus station east of the temple.

Irinjalakuda
Irinjalakuda's **Natana Kairali Research and Performing Centre** is dedicated to the performance, preservation, documentation and promotion of Kerala's performing arts, particularly Koodiyattam (theatre), Nangiar Koothu (solo performance) and puppetry.

Performances are held here from time to time, especially during the centre's 12-day annual festival.

The renovated **Koodalmanikyam Temple** (*Tel: 0480 282 6631. www.koodalmanikyam.com. Open: daily 3–11.30am & 5–8.15pm*) at Irinjalakuda is an unusual temple dedicated to Rama's brother Bharata, and depicting his joy when he learned of the victory of Rama and his reunion with Sita. Irinjalakuda is also home to the **Church of St Thomas** (*Tel: 0480 282 6376. Open: daily 6am–6pm*), an impressive building erected in 1917 on the site of an older church dating from 1845. In January the images of saints are taken out in procession, accompanied by firework displays. *16km (10 miles) south of Thrissur. For information about courses at Natana Kairali Research & Performing Centre for Traditional Arts contact the director at Venu G, Natana Kairali, Ammanur Chakyar Madhom, Irinjalakuda 680121. Tel: 0480 282 5559. www.natanakaisiki.mimemo.net*

Kalady

Kalady, by the River Periyar, is the birthplace of Sankaracharya, one of the most important philosophers in India. In the 8th century, Sankaracharya founded the Advaita Vedanta, which has spread throughout Southern India and to other parts of the country. Kalady has two shrines in his memory, as well as a tower with details about his life and the Advainta ways of worship. *10km (6 miles) northeast of Kochi.*

Kerala Kalamandalam

Founded in the 1920s and 1930s by the poet Vellathol Menon and his associate Mukunda Raja, this is an important academy for teaching the performing arts of Kerala, particularly Kathakali, Mohiniattam, Koodiyattam and Ottan Thullal. The centre is credited with the revival of Kerala's dance forms and for opening its doors to Hindus and non-Hindus alike, and it has also established international links for the promotion of Kathakali overseas. Located 16km (10 miles) north of Thrissur in Cheruthuruthy, the campus's pleasant buildings include a theatre which is designed in the style of the performing halls of Kerala's temples. *Tel: 0488 4262 418. www.kalamandalam.org. Open: 9am–noon & 2–5pm on working days. The office can give information on the performances and courses on offer. Send an email to info@kalamandalam.org for interaction with the masters and for information on courses at Kerala Kalamandalam.*

Megalithic sites

Huge stone monuments are among the earliest evidence of settlement in Kerala. Some of the best megalithic sites are located near Guruvayoor, while Chovannur has a sizeable number of the 'hat-stones' (locally called *topi-kals*) that are distinctive Iron-Age megalithic remains. Substantial remnants of Kerala's megalithic era can also be seen at Porkalam, near Thrissur.

Classical dances

Southern India is known for its living tradition of classical dances. The most popular is probably the Bharatanatyam of Tamil Nadu, which is a graceful and highly stylised form of dance usually performed by women. It combines music, gestures and mime with pure dance and expression, usually on themes of true love. A traditional recital begins with a floral offering to a deity and the first section of the performance is the *Alarippu*, which is based on the rhythm of drum beats and the vocals

Traditional Indian dancers

of the conductor. The central section is *Varnam*, which is physically and emotionally demanding as the dancer shows her skill, dancing to the rhythm, moods and music. The final stage, called *Tillana*, shows the dancer reverting to rhythm as the performance nears its end with a concluding prayer.

The main elements of Kathakali are the sung narrative, the accompaniment of percussion instruments and the danced mime. The performer uses a variety of gestures and steps to portray the narrative, which is sung as the background theme of the performance. Boys are recruited at a very young age and spend seven or more years learning the *mudras*, hand and finger gestures and movements of the neck, head, tongue, eyes, feet, toes, arms and hands.

Mohiniattam, the dance of the enchantress, is a sensuous solo female performance that evokes the mood of love. The dance is dedicated to the female incarnation of Vishnu, Mohini the enchantress, who gives pleasure to the virtuous and brings destruction to the immoral.

Kuchipudi is a dance form of Andhra that is similar to Bharatanatyam and follows the Natya Shastras very closely. It is generally considered a folk idiom that is freer and more flexible than most other classical dance forms of Southern India. The dance drama presents an episode or a series of episodes, usually from Hindu epics, and usually performed by a group of men (though there are also solo versions). As well as mime and pure dance, Kuchipudi may also use speech in the drama.

Ottan Thullal is a male solo performance that depicts topical issues. Its simplicity, humour and satire have made it a popular art in Kerala. The dancer enacts the script with gestures, movements and expression.

Koothu, a solo performance, and Koodiyattam (sometimes spelt Kutiyattam), a group performance, are ancient Sanskrit dramas believed to be the inspiration behind the growth of dance dramas like Kathakali in Kerala. The Krishnanattam, patronised by the Raja Manaveda, the Zamorin of Kozhikode in the mid-17th century, has become a ritual dance at the Krishna temple of Guruvayoor, enacting the life of Krishna. Ramanattam is a similar performance, dedicated to the life of Rama.

Yakshagana from Karnataka is as much a musical play as a dance. The troupe dons elaborate make-up and costumes for the drama, which also allows the performers to speak and develop dialogue.

PERIYAR
Periyar National Park

The park is one of Kerala's most popular tourist destinations. The reserve's artificial lake was created in 1895 by British engineers in order to irrigate Madurai and Ramanathapuram districts and to provide water to the city of Madurai. The dam submerged prime forests but resulted in the Maharaja of Travancore protecting the richly vegetated hills adjoining the lake.

Periyar is 110km (69 miles) southeast of Kochi. There is a tourist information office at Aranya Nivas in the park (Tel: 0486 922 2023. aranyanivas@sancharnet.in), and the Wildlife Information Centre at Thekkady (Tel: 0486 922 2028) can be contacted for details about viewing facilities.

Periyar Tiger Reserve

This sanctuary was established by the Travancore State in 1934 and became part of 'Project Tiger' in 1973. Although Periyar is a tiger reserve, it is more famous for its elephants, which can be seen from the tourist launches that operate two-hour trips on the lake. Elephants come to the lake to drink and to feed on the marshy grasslands. Gaur (Indian bison), sambar deer, wild boar and Nilgiri langurs are common here, and lucky visitors may also see sloth bears, dholes (wild dogs), otters and the endangered lion-tailed macaque. This is a good spot for birdwatching, with species such as darter, cormorant, osprey, stork and kingfisher.

Guided nature treks depart from the information centre and last about three hours. On these treks you are likely to see barking deer, Malabar giant squirrels, monkeys such as langurs and bonnet macaques, great and grey hornbills, grey jungle fowl, mynahs, orioles, racket-tailed drongos and monitor lizards. Some tourists come face to face with elephant herds, and watchtowers and viewing platforms can also be used, for a fee.

More serious treks, such as the Tiger Trails (an eco-development project), are also possible and include camping and staying at watchtowers in the forests. These treks cover habitats like the grasslands, where the mega-herbivores are usually seen, the moist deciduous forests and the semi-evergreen and evergreen forests. Tiger and panther sightings are rare, but visitors can see a number of other mammals, as well as an interesting variety of birds and butterflies.

Periyar Tiger Reserve. Tel: 0486 922 4571. www.periyartigerreserve.org; mail@periyartigerreserve.org. Admission charge.

Two-hour launch cruises, called boat safaris, depart from the jetty at regular intervals. The first cruise runs from 7–9am, and the last from 4–6pm. The guided nature trek starts at 7am.

Plantations

Some spice plantations near Periyar Tiger Reserve welcome visitors, and tourist offices, spice shops and some hotels run guided tours to the cardamom, rubber and coffee plantations of Murikkady, the pepper plantations at Vandiperiyar and the cardamom centre at Vandanmedu. Peermade (sometimes spelt Pirmed), on the road from Kottayam to Kumily leading to Periyar Tiger Reserve, has a number of picturesquely located tea, rubber and cardamom plantations. *Most hotels and resorts at Thekkady, Kumily, Vandanmedu and Pirmed can arrange visits to plantations.*

Temples

There are a number of temples near Periyar Tiger Reserve. One of the best known is Mangaladevi Temple, situated on the crest of a hill, but it is now largely neglected and is only open for certain festivals. Permission is required from the forest department office at Thekkady to visit this temple.

Wildlife Information Centre, Periyar Tiger Reserve, PO Kumily, Thekkady. Tel: 0486 922 2028.

Elephants roam freely around Periyar National Park

MUNNAR
Munnar town

At 1,652m (5,420ft), Munnar is a popular hill resort for visitors to Kerala. It is a small town with a spectacular setting near Anamudi, South India's highest peak. The abbreviation of two Tamil words, *moonu* (three) and *aar* (river), Munnar lies at the confluence of the Kuthirappuzha, Nallathanni and Kundala rivers.

Like other hill stations of India, the small town of Munnar was discovered and established by the British to serve the needs of some of the world's highest tea plantations. Until the late 19th century, it was a deeply forested area inhabited mainly by tribal groups like the Madhuvans.

The growth of Munnar as the commercial centre of tea estates began in 1887 with the opening of the High Ranges of Travancore, also called the Kannan Devan Hills, for agriculture. An official of Travancore, Munro, was the first to lease the hill tracts for agriculture. After experimenting with rubber, chichona and other crops, the planters found the area suitable for the cultivation of tea. The giant tea company of James Finlay & Co was established in 1895 and eventually controlled most of the tea estates around Munnar. Access to Munnar was by train from Tamil Nadu until 1931 when a road was opened from Kochi, making life easier for the planters.

In 1964, the Finlay estates went into a joint venture with the Tatas, one of India's wealthiest families. Today, Tata Tea controls most of the tea production around Munnar and is among the largest producers in India. The tea from their Kannan Devan Estate is especially famous.

Munnar still has colonial buildings, including old bungalows, and recreational life is focused around the clubs which were set up for British planters.

Munnar is 304km (190 miles) northeast of Thiruvananthapuram, 153km (95 miles) east of Kochi and 287km (179 miles) southeast of Kozhikode.

Christ Church

This Protestant church, built in 1910, is set on a hill near the town centre. It has a pleasant interior which is notable for its stained-glass windows, and its original pews can still be seen. The cemetery on the hillside above the church is older, with tombs dating from 1894 and brass plaques in honour of the planters.

This church is in Old Munnar and has services in Tamil and Malayalam. The Christmas Mass is popular. Open: daily 7am–5pm.

Tata Tea Museum

Old equipment and photographs documenting the tea-making process are on show at this museum. Thirsty visitors can also take part in some tasting.

1.5km (1 mile) north of town centre. Open: daily 10am–5pm. Admission charge.

Munnar environs
Devikulam

Devikulam has beautiful views over the high ranges of the Western Ghats. Devikulam Lake is in a private estate and you will need permission from the Tata office in Munnar (*Near Citibank. Tel: 0486 523 0561.* *www.tatatea.com*) to visit it. The lake is particularly beautiful – locals believe that Sita bathed at the lake, and so they consider it to be holy and possess curative powers. The name Devikulam means 'the lake of the goddess'.

15km (9 miles) from Munnar town.

Kerala

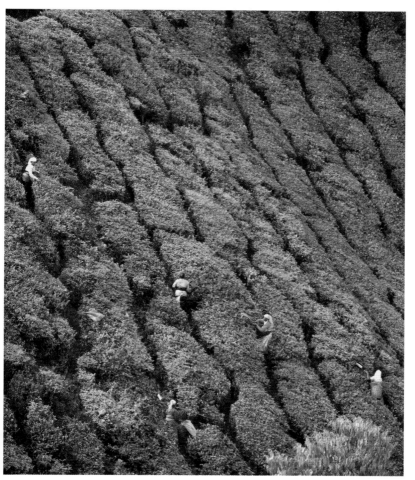

Tea pickers on steep slopes at Munnar

Tour: Munnar to Top Station

Most visitors to Munnar come to explore the surrounding hills with their neatly manicured tea estates and forests. One of the prettiest routes is the drive from Munnar to Top Station, with its high-altitude tea estates, as well as flowering plants such as Neelakurinji, an orchid that blooms every 12 years, covering the mountain sides with colour.

Although the distance from Munnar to Top Station is only about 34km (21 miles), you need to allow 4–5 hours for the return trip, as the mountain roads are slow going. It is also a good idea to check on the road conditions before

setting off: during the rainy season fallen trees are not uncommon.

Take the road from Munnar to Top Station, leading past tea estates, some of which have retail outlets. It may be

An old British-style tea station at Munnar

possible to obtain permission to visit one of the tea estates and see a working factory. Plantation activities such as tea picking can be seen from the road on working days.

1 Mattupetty Lake

At an altitude of 1,700m (5,577ft), this huge lake was created by a hydroelectric project. It has been developed as a tourist attraction, and facilities include speedboat rides and horse riding. Elephants and wild boar are sometimes seen in the surrounding forests.

3km (2 miles) after Mattupetty, you will see the entrance of the Indo-Swiss dairy project, which is now run by the Kerala Livestock Development Board as a cattle breeding and research centre. From here the road rises to Kundaly.

2 Kundaly

The dam at Kundaly is a few hundred metres off the road. Full of trout and other fish, it has a beautiful setting in the hills and is surrounded by grasslands

and forests, where elephants and gaur (Indian bison) can sometimes be spotted. An old colonial inspection bungalow stands in the woods near the lake's shore. Four kilometres (2¹/₂ miles) from the dam is a golf course (*Top Station, Munnar*), with an attractive clubhouse, administered by Tata Tea for planters and guests. Permission is required for a visit or a game and the last stretch of road requires a jeep. *After Kundaly, the road ascends to Top Station.*

3 Top Station

At 2,200m (7,218ft), Top Station, on the border of Tamil Nadu, has a great view of some of India's highest tea plantations. Little now remains of the ropeway that was used to transport tea to the valley floor, called Lower Station.

From Top Station you can return to Munnar. Some travellers may wish to use this route to travel on to Kodaikanal, a hill station in Tamil Nadu.

Tour: Wildlife trail from Munnar to Chinnar

The 60km (37-mile) route from Munnar to Chinnar Wildlife Sanctuary, at the Tamil Nadu border, is great for seeing a variety of endangered flora and fauna from the sandalwood tree to the Nilgiri tahr.

This is a full-day tour and an early start is necessary as the roads are hilly, and some walking is involved at Rajmalai, Marayoor and Chinnar.

Take the road north from Munnar to Rajmalai, and turn left from the main road about 14km (9 miles) from Munnar.

1 Eravikulam National Park

The park is home to the endangered Nilgiri tahr, a relative of the domestic goat, which has erect ears, long sturdy limbs and rounded horns that end in an impressive curving sweep. It does not have the beard and twisted horns of a goat, but it is just as agile and sure-footed.

Designated a national park in 1978, Eravikulam was previously set up as a sanctuary for the protection of the Nilgiri tahr. Spanning an area of 97sq km (37sq miles) of *shola* habitat, comprising rolling grassland and forest, the park contains the high peak of Mt Anamudi (2,695m/8,842ft). Besides Nilgiri tahr, Eravikulam is also the home of elephants, tigers, panthers, wild dogs, Nilgiri langurs, lion-tailed macaques and giant squirrels. Regular

buses are the only way to enter the park; foreign tourists are charged extra and are therefore allowed to queue jump. The goats are easily spotted, and you will be able to see a variety of birds.

Eravikulam National Park.
Tel: 0486 523 1587. www.eravikulam.org; roywlw@eravikulam.org. Open: Sept–May daily 7am–6pm. Admission charge.
Return to the highway and drive north past tea estates and a Hindu shrine. To the left is Marayoor village.

A Nilgiri tahr in Eravikulam National Park

2 Marayoor

This natural sandalwood forest is the only substantial one left in Kerala, and it is strictly protected. Only dead and diseased trees are removed. The forest officer may be able to arrange treks with Tamil tribal guides. Marayoor has important megalithic sites and prehistoric rock paintings, but be warned that the trek to this particular site is strenuous.
www.marayoor.com.

From Marayoor, the road continues 20km (12 miles) to Chinnar Wildlife Sanctuary. Langurs, bonnet macaques and peafowl are often seen from the road. Just off the main road is a watchtower, which is great for viewing wildlife.

3 Chinnar Wildlife Sanctuary

This 90sq km (35sq mile) reserve, which is currently under consideration for selection as a UNESCO World Heritage Site, contains a range of habitats, from *shola* forest and grasslands in the hills to drier forests in the rain shadow region. There are elephants, gaur, deer and panthers, as well as the rare grizzled giant squirrel. A good variety of birds and butterflies can be seen along the path to the watchtower.
Chinnar Wildlife Sanctuary. Tel: 0486 523 1587; enpmunnar@sify.com.
Open: daily 7am–6pm. Admission charge. The drive from the entrance of Chinnar Wildlife Sanctuary direct to Munnar is 52km (32 miles), but expect to spend 3–4 hours on the road.

KOZHIKODE
Kozhikode city

Mentioned in the writings of Marco Polo, Kozhikode's moniker, the 'city of spices', alludes to its importance in the spice trade of yore. The place's historical significance also included a stint as the main port on the Malabar Coast. Close by is the beach where famed Portuguese explorer Vasco da Gama and his men first touched down on Indian soil in 1498.

Its glory days may have waned since that pivotal footfall, but Kozhikode has retained some of its commercial functions. Spices are still traded here with vigour, with coconuts also big business, while timber dealing, boat building and construction continue apace. All this lends the former capital an industrious atmosphere. The presence of one of Kerala's three airports also contributes to the hum of activity. That is not to say that the town – the state's third largest – is all workaday grime. Indeed, one research firm recently rated it the second-best Indian city in which to live.

Without the beach scene found further south or the cluster of attractions of Kochi, Kozhikode (sometimes still referred to by its British name of Calicut) does not attract as many foreign visitors as certain other Keralan towns. But this can work in its favour for travellers who appreciate more authentic destinations, with fewer chances of running into fellow tourists at every juncture. The town's large and attractive beach sees few enough foreign faces that your arrival will still prompt curious conversation from local people.

Like much of the northern reaches of Kerala, the Muslim minority has made its presence felt here, both architecturally and culturally. This much is apparent if you take the time to wander through some of the city's meandering little back streets, a leisurely way to get the feel of Kozhikode's historical atmosphere. *Kozhikode is 382km (237 miles) northwest of Thiruvananthapuram and 188km (117 miles) from Kochi, with good road and rail connections. It also has an international airport.*

Mananchira

Little remains of the Zamorin's old royal enclave at Mananchira. Locals believe the Zamorin killed himself in his palace, rather than face defeat at the hands of the Mysorean Sultans after peace talks failed. Temples, mosques and churches surround the square.

Mosques

The Kuttichara area of Kozhikode is known for its medieval mosques. The four-storey **Mishkal Mosque** is in the traditional Kerala style, with gabled roof and wooden columns; partly burned by the Portuguese in 1510, most of the original building still stands. Another mosque in the traditional style is the **Muccunti Palli**, which has a slab stating that the land was a donation from the Zamorin.

The mosques are within walking distance of each other.

Museums

The **Pazhassiraja Museum** has interesting models of different kinds of megalithic monuments of Kerala and replicas of Hindu temples, as well as collections of coins, bronzes and copies of original murals. Next door, the **Krishna Menon Museum** (*Tel: 0495 238 1253*) has clothes, speeches and photographs of this former defence minister of India, while the Art Gallery in the same building has an excellent collection of paintings by Indian artists, including Raja Varma.

The museums are on East Hill about 5km (3 miles) from the city centre. Pazhassiraja Museum. Open: Tue–Sun 10am–5pm. Krisha Menon Museum and Art Gallery. Open: Tue & Thur–Sun 10am–5pm, Wed 1–5pm. Admission charge.

Tali Temple

This temple is known for its woodcarvings and huge statues of the

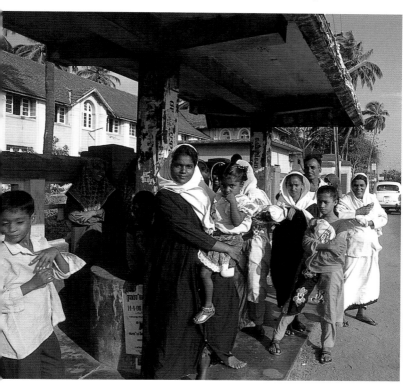

Muslim women and children wait at a bus stop in Kozhikode

deities. Probably dating from the reign of the Zamorin, it is now an important religious centre in Kozhikode.

The temple is south of the city centre. Open to Hindus only.

Kozhikode environs

Beypore

Beypore has been a shipbuilding centre for many centuries. Today, its yards produce hand-built dhows called *urus*, which are exported to the Gulf countries. Visitors can buy miniature replicas. Beypore is also known for its Tasara Creative Weaving Centre (*www.tasaraindia.com*) which trains artisans in textile skills.

8km (5 miles) south of Kozhikode.

Kadalundi Bird Sanctuary

This bird sanctuary at the estuary of the Kadalundi River has a number of resident species of kingfishers, herons and gulls. It is best visited in winter when flocks of migrants come here.

The sanctuary is on two sides of the river 19km (12 miles) south of Kozhikode. Opening hours variable.

Kappad

Kappad has a stone memorial marking the spot where Vasco da Gama is said to have landed in 1498. The beach at Kappad is popular with day trippers from Kozhikode, as the city's own beaches are rather crowded.

About 16km (10 miles) north of Kozhikode.

Kottakal

Kottakal is home to the Arya Vaidya Sala Hospital, which is regarded as one of India's most renowned

Wind-drying a saree on Kappad Beach

The Vasco da Gama memorial pillar at Kappad

Ayurvedic centres, and which has been involved in research and practice for more than 100 years.

48km (30 miles) south of Kozhikode. Arya Vaidya Sala, Kottakal. Tel: 0483 274 2216. www.aryavaidyasala.com; mail@aryavaidyasala.com

Mahe

Mahe has an interesting colonial history, first under the British and then as a French colony under Pondicherry. The French arrived at Malabar in the 17th century to establish its spice-trading base. Located on a hill and overlooking a river, the town was named after Mahé de Labourdonnais who conquered it in 1725. Handed over to the Government of India in 1958, Mahe has few remnants of its French colonial history, one exception being

St Theresa's Church (*Tel: 0490 233 2332. Open: 6.45am–9.30pm*). The town also has an arts institution, the **Malayala Kalagramam Centre for Arts and Ideas**, which offers courses in music, dance, sculpture and painting.
60km (37 miles) from Kozhikode towards Kannur. For information about courses contact Malayala Kala. Tel: 0490 233 2961.

Vadakara

The **Lokarnarkavu Temple Complex** (*open to Hindus only*) is 5km (3 miles) from the town centre of Vadakara. It has three temples, with the oldest and biggest dedicated to Durga and the others to Vishnu and Shiva, as well as a number of rock caves and tanks. The temples have attractive carvings near the entrance and some interesting paintings inside.
Vadakara is on National Highway 17.

KANNUR
Kannur city

Kannur, or Cannanore, was an important spice-trading port, visited by the likes of Marco Polo. Ruled for centuries by the Kolatri Rajas, European powers began to exert their influence from the 15th century. The Portuguese made it a military base, building a fort which took advantage of Kannur's position on raised ground above cliffs facing the sea.

After a period of Dutch rule, Kannur became an important British centre in 1790. Besides the buildings erected by the Europeans, it also has some old quarters of the local Moplah (Mapilla) Muslim trading community.

Kannur is 278km (173 miles) northwest of Kochi, 90km (56 miles) northwest of Kozhikode and 465km (289 miles) northwest of Thiruvananthapuram, with good rail connections to these cities, and to Mumbai, Delhi and other major Indian cities.

Beaches

Kannur has a number of beaches, although none of them is particularly well known as a tourist destination. The most popular is **Payyambalam Beach**, near the fort.

St Angelo Fort

This fort was built by the Portuguese in 1505 during the Viceregalship of Almeida. The Dutch occupied the fort in 1663 and sold it in 1772 to the Ali Raja of Kannur, who was the first Muslim ruler of Kerala. Ali Raja had a short tenure, before the British conquest of 1790 made St Angelo Fort one of the most important British army bases in South India. Built from laterite blocks, the fort walls are protected by the sea, and by a moat on the landward side. The British practically rebuilt the rest of the fort within the walls for their garrisons, and some of the old cannons still stand, but the highlight of a visit to the fort is the view of the sea, and occasionally of the fishing fleet returning with their catch.

Open: daily 8am–6pm.
Free admission, but there is a small charge to park.

Kannur environs
Chirakkal

This was the capital of the Kolatri Rajas when they ruled Kannur, and the wooden mansion that served as their palace can be seen here. Chirakkal also has some interesting temples.

6km (4 miles) from Kannur.

Parassinikkadavu Temple

This temple rises on the banks of the Valapatanam and is associated with the legend of Muthapan, the hunter form of Lord Shiva, who is said to have appeared before (or been born to) a Shiva-worshipping childless couple. As a hunter, Muthapan did not appeal to the family, so Shiva appeared before them in his divine form. He was fond of toddy, and was given it whenever he

Parassinikkadavu Temple, near Kannur

was called upon to perform a miracle, which is why toddy remains the main offering at the temple.

The non-conformist temple has always been open to all castes, and to non-Hindus as well. The main tourist attraction is to attend the dawn and dusk Teyyam performance which opens and closes the temple ceremonies. The Teyyam here portrays the legend of Muthapan, said to have selected Parassinikkadavu as his sacred home. Muthapan is depicted with a dog as a companion, and therefore street dogs are welcomed and offered toddy and fish. *The temple is about 18km (11 miles) from Kannur. Open: daily 5–8am &*

6.30–8.30pm. Teyyam *is performed daily at 6.30am & 5.45pm. Donation appreciated.*

Sri Thrikkaikunnu Mahadeva Temple
One of the largest of its kind, the Sri Thrikkaikunnu Mahadeva Temple showcases a pure form of Keralan architecture. The wooden carvings about the building portray scenes from Hindu mythology, and the site boasts sculptures that date back up to two centuries. *The temple is at Kottayam Malabar, about 8km (5 miles) northeast of Thalasseri (see pp76–7). Tel: 0490 236 3700. www.srithrikkaikunnu.org. Opening hours variable.*

Cottage industries

Called the 'Land of Loom and Lore', Kannur is known for its handloom-weaving industry that is said to date back to the 16th century. The success story of its handloom exports over the last 50 years or so has earned it recognition from the Government of India as a 'Town of Export Excellence', and a long-mooted textile park near Kannur to make the most of its expertise is now slowly taking shape. From traditional sarees and sarongs, the weaving units and handloom cooperatives have now diversified into home furnishings for the export market. About 100,000 people in Kannur district are employed by the textile sector.

It is possible to view the entire process from spinning to weaving to dyeing – just ask permission in the office. The Kanhirode Handloom Weaver's Cooperative Society (*Tel: 0497 285 7259*) is one of the oldest, established in 1952, and it turns out cotton and silk fabrics, soft furnishings, sarees and *dhotis* (sarongs). In 2002 it set up a common facility centre for other units in the district that lacked dyeing equipment and other infrastructure, making this one of the best places to see the many stages of Kannur's textile industry. The cooperative has many different kinds of loom, including a 2.3m (91-inch) Malabar loom. Many

Deft finger work is required in the workers' cooperatives

of the cooperatives also have retail centres where visitors can buy shirts, fabrics and furnishings.

At the Kerala Dinesh Beedi Workers' Cooperative (*Tel: 0497 270 1699; www.keraladinesh.com*) near Kannur you can see workers making *beedis*, the local cigarettes that are popular in India. Owned and managed by the workers and retirees, most of them women, the government supports the cooperative's aims, which are to improve the income of *beedi* workers and to give them better working conditions than elsewhere. Most of the workers are 'rollers', who cut the leaves before filling them with tobacco and rolling them into reefers. The *beedis* are then tied into bundles and sent to the packing and shipping departments.

Selling garlands in Thiruvananthapuram

An important feature of the unit, embodying the literacy and political awareness of the people of Kerala, is the 'reader' who reads aloud from the local newspapers so that the workers can hear. There are also meals and washroom facilities, and workers are entitled to leave allowance, gratuities and a retirement pension. The purchasing, marketing and financial accounting departments are centralised for all the production units in the cooperative. Although the cooperative has been successful in improving the conditions of Kerala's

beedi workers and has sustained profitability for most of the years of operation, it has fallen on somewhat harder times since smoking has been banned in a number of public places.

The cooperative has worked on other projects such as agro-processing, making and packaging curry powders, pickles, coconut cream, jams and other popular food products. There has also been a move into information technology, which has established data-entry training centres and entire software business parks with development centres, networks, computer labs and design centres, a library, and internet and counselling facilities. However, the income has not been enough to sustain employment. The government has bailed out the workers at the cooperative, incurring protests from the private sector.

Tour: Kannur to Thalasseri

This 22km (14-mile) tour covers the attractions on National Highway 17 between Kannur and Thalasseri, known for their forts. It also takes in some key historical sites, as well as something that may come as a surprise to foreign tourists: a 'drive-on' beach!

Allow about 4–5 hours for the return trip.

Take National Highway 17 south from Kannur to Thalasseri. After 8km (5 miles) you will come to an unpaved road to the right, which winds through coconut palms to Muzhappilangad Beach.

1 Muzhappilangad Beach

This is one of the finest beaches in Kerala, stretching for 4km (2½ miles) along a bay with a wide strip of white sand. The palm trees to the north and the rocks to the south make it ideal for photographs of picture-postcard sunsets. However, the Muzhappilangad is being promoted as a 'drive-on' beach by the tourist authorities, and so it can get very crowded during holidays. *Continue on National Highway 17 for about 3km (2 miles) to Illikunnu, just off the highway.*

2 Illikunnu

German missionary Herman Gundert settled at Illikunnu in 1889 and stayed for about three decades. It was here that he wrote the first Malayalam journal and the first Malayalam–English dictionary. The house is in typical Keralan style but is closed for public viewing.
Return from the house to the highway and drive to Thalasseri.

3 Thalasseri

Thalasseri, or Tellicherry, was one of the most important British military bases in Malabar, and it was the site of their first factory there. The Raja of Chirakkal permitted the British to build the fort at Thalasseri to protect their interests in spices along the coast and in the hill plantations. The fort was built in 1708 and successfully withstood the struggle between the British and the Mysorean sultans.

Entered by an impressive gate flanked by comical images of guards, the fort has high walls and an abandoned lighthouse, and there are many tales of the secret underground tunnels leading from the fort. Behind it are other colonial buildings, including two churches and a school. The cemetery contains the grave of Edward Brennan, who was the founder of Brennan College, a highly respected institution.

Thalasseri also has old Moplah houses of the Muslim merchant families. Their mosque is in traditional Malabari style, and local accounts say it dates to the 16th century. Thalasseri is also known for its gymnastics school, run by the national sports authority, and for its kalari centre, which instructs students in the traditional martial arts of Kerala.
It is an 11km (7-mile) drive from Thalasseri back to Kannur.

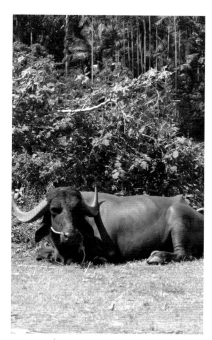
Bull at the roadside near Kannur

KASARAGOD
Kasaragod city

The name of the northernmost district of Kerala derives its name from the Sanskrit for 'land of lakes'. Ruled by the Nayakas, Kasaragod town fell to Tipu Sultan and came under British rule after the Mysore Wars. It now has a large Muslim population and is known for its mosques, but also has many interesting temples and lovely beaches, so is becoming a tourist centre. *Kasaragod is 344km (214 miles) from Kochi, 156km (97 miles) from Kozhikode and 560km (348 miles) from Thiruvananthapuram, with good train connections.*

Mosques

With a large Muslim population, the town has many mosques, including the beautiful **Malik Deenar Jumma Masjid**, built in Keralan style and believed to be the burial site of Malik Ibn Dinar.

Thalangara, 800m (½ mile) south of Kasaragod station, by Chandragiri River. www.malikdeenarmasjid.com. Open: daily 6am–8pm.

Kasaragod environs
Anantha Padmanabha Temple

This temple is believed to date from the 9th century, although the present structure is more recent, and it is venerated as the original abode of Padmanabhaswamy, the deity of Thiruvananthapuram. Set in a small lake, the temple has a bridge connecting the *gopuram*, or gatehouse, and the sanctuary. The principal deity, Vishnu, is shown sitting on the serpent Anantha, and not reclining as in the more famous Padmanabhaswamy Temple at Thiruvananthapuram. The murals depicting Puranic themes have been recently restored to their former glory. *The temple is east of Kasaragod town. Open to Hindus only.*

PUPPETRY IN KERALA

Yakshagana Bombeyatta is a form of puppetry that now, sadly, has few practitioners, although some can still be seen in Kasaragod. It is based on the Yakshagana folk theatre of Karnataka, and uses song and elaborately costumed puppets to relate tales from the Hindu epics. String puppets and rod puppets are used, and their costumes and movements enact the role of the character in the story. Sri Gopalakrishna Yakshagana Bombeyatta Sanga at Kasaragod is an organisation promoting and performing this folk art.

Puppetry also survives as a performing art form in Palakkad district, and the village of Partithupuli is home to the Adi Pandaram puppeteers who came to Kerala from Andhra Pradesh. Despite its origins in Telugu, the language of Andhra Pradesh, this form of glove puppetry is influenced by Pavakathali, the Kathakali dance drama. Pavakathali employs painted puppets decorated with peacock feathers to portray scenes from the *Mahabharata* and other epics.

Tolpava Koothu, literally 'leather puppet play', enacts tales from the *Ramayana* by projecting shadows of leather puppets onto a white background. This is a ritualised folk art performed on a stage facing the deity, Kali, and 100 or so puppets can be used in a single performance.

The Malik Deenar Jumma Masjid (mosque), said to be the burial site of Malik Ibn Dinar

Bekal

Bekal is famous for its fort, which offers superb views of the sea. Originally said to be part of the Kadamba kingdom, Bekal passed on to the Vijayanagara dynasty and the Kolatri Rajas. The fort was probably built in the 17th century when the Nayakas took Bekal after the decline of Vijayanagara. Tipu Sultan took Bekal, and the British occupied the fort after they defeated the sultan. The walls of the fort are still intact, and a tunnel leads from the interior directly to the sea.

Dedicated to Hanuman, Anjaneya Temple is built against the fort walls, while south of the fort is Bekal Beach. Six kilometres (4 miles) from the fort is another good beach, at Kappil.
The fort is 80km (50 miles) northwest of Kannur. Tel: 0467 227 2900. Open: daily 8am–5pm. Nominal admission fee and a video camera charge.

Chandragiri Fort

This is one of a string of fortresses built along the coast by the Nayakas in the 17th century. Though largely neglected, the fort has lovely sea views.
3km (2 miles) south of Kasaragod.

Kottancherry

Kottancherry is a pleasant place for walks in the Western Ghats.
52km (32 miles) southeast of Kasaragod.

Nileshwar

Nileshwar is known for its government-approved yoga institute (*www.neeleshwarhermitage.com*). *Nileshwar is south of Kasaragod past Bekal towards Kannur.*

WAYANAD

Wayanad is one of the most forested districts of Kerala, and it has a high tribal population. The district is also known for its waterfalls and wildlife. The name, Wayanad, is believed to be a shortened version of the word *Valnadu*, meaning 'land of paddy', and the local economy thrives on rice fields, tea, coffee and spice plantations.

The headquarters of Wayanad district is Kalpetta, 251km (156 miles) north of Kochi, 63km (39 miles) northeast of Kozhikode and 467km (290 miles) from Thiruvananthapuram.

Edakkal

The **Edakkal Caves** comprise Kerala's most famous prehistoric site, featuring petroglyphs sculpted into the rocks. The drawings are formed by geometric lines and are generally dated to about 10,000 BC. Some scripts are said to be dated from the 3rd century BC. There are also good views of the surrounding hills.

Ancient tombstones in the Mananthavadi churchyard

12km (7½ miles) from Sultan's Bathery. Tel: 0493 622 1860. www.edakkal.com; info@edakkal.com. Open: daily 9am–5pm. Admission charge.

Heritage Museum

This museum exhibits archaeological finds from the district, mainly 14th- to 16th-century sculptures of deities, as well as tribal artefacts such as local jewellery, weapons and fish traps, and agricultural implements.

Ambalavayal, 25km (15½ miles) from Kalpetta. Open: daily 9am–5pm. Admission charge.

Mananthavadi

Mananthavadi has a 19th-century church (*opening hours variable*) that serves the Christian converts among the local tribal population, especially the Kuruchiyas. The churchyard has some old tombstones.

32km (20 miles) north of Kalpetta.

Plantations

Wayanad has a number of tea, coffee and spice plantations. The district is also one of the highest producers of areca nuts (betelnuts).

Hotels and resorts at Vythri and Kalpetta arrange plantation visits.

Pookot

Pookot has a lake that has been developed for recreational tourism with boating facilities.

63km (39 miles) from Kozhikode. Open: 9am–6pm. Admission charge.

Sultan's Bathery

This town is named after Tipu Sultan, but there are few signs of the sultan's fort which the British destroyed. There is a **Jain temple** in the town which probably dates from the 12th or 13th century, and which has carved ceilings. *98km (61 miles) northeast of Kozhikode. Regular buses from Mysore, Kalpetta and Kozhikode. Sultan's Bathery has hotels and restaurants.*

Thirunelly

Thirunelly has an important Vishnu Temple, sometimes called 'the Kashi of Kerala'. Devotees bathe in a mountain stream called Papanasini, which they believe brings visitors eternal bliss. *North of Kalpetta via Mananthavadi. Open: sunrise–sunset.*

Wildlife reserves

Wayanad Wildlife Sanctuary forms part of the **Nilgiri Biosphere Reserve**. Access is from Tholpetty near Mananthavadi in the north, or from Muthunga near Sultan's Bathery in the south. Across the border in Karnataka, **Nagarhole** or **Rajiv Gandhi National Park** can be accessed from Karapur near Mananthavadi and **Bandipur National Park** by continuing on the road past the Muthunga entrance. You are likely to see elephants, sambar deer, spotted and barking deer, gaur or Indian bison, wild boar, Hanuman langurs and bonnet macaques. Fortunate visitors could spot sloth bears, but tiger, panther and dhole

The Jain temple at Sultan's Bathery

(wild dog) sightings are rare. Mastigudi in Nagarhole is a good place to see large herds of elephants during the dry months. These forests are also rich in birdlife, including grey jungle fowl, red spurfowl, Malabar pied hornbills, hill mynahs, crested serpent eagles and hawk eagles. Wetland birds can be seen along the Kabini River.

A permit for the Wayanad sanctuaries can be obtained from Muthunga, Kalpetta or Tholpetty. Admission, vehicle entry, guide and camera charges are paid to the local forest officer. There are usually jeeps at the forest department offices for hire to visit the sanctuary. Nagarhole. Tel: 0821 248 0901. Open: daily 6–8am & 3–5.30pm. Admission charge. Bandipur National Park. Open: daily 6–9am & 4–6pm (approx.). Admission charge.

Karnataka

Karnataka is perhaps the most diverse of the four states of Southern India. It has varied scenery, from the long coastline and forested hills to the ancient rocky outcrops of the Deccan Plateau, as well as a rich architectural legacy of 5th- to 12th-century temples, medieval mosques, the eclectic palaces of Mysore, and numerous forts. Its cultural diversity encompasses the tribal villages in the hills, and the traditional temple towns, as well as the modern, cosmopolitan atmosphere of Bangalore.

Bordering Goa, Maharashtra, Andhra Pradesh, Tamil Nadu and Kerala, with a coastline along the Arabian Sea, Karnataka is a relatively large state, both in terms of geographical size and population. In order to attract more foreign tourists, it is currently being enthusiastically marketed under the tagline 'one state, many worlds' – an apposite encapsulation of its diversity.

The coast of Karnataka has many fine beaches and mangrove estuaries, while the hills are among the wettest areas of the Western Ghats. Here you will find spectacular waterfalls, along with the headwaters of great rivers such as the Krishna, the Kaveri (also spelt Cauvery) and the Tungabhadra, as well as forests rich in wildlife. Much of the state falls in the Deccan Plateau, where some of the world's oldest granite and other ancient rock formations can be found.

The main urban hub is Bangalore, or Bengaluru, to which it is currently in the process of being renamed. India's third most populous city continues to grow, buoyed by a vibrant IT industry, which has led it to be dubbed the Silicon Valley of India.

While the capital is thriving on the back of the modern, Karnataka is also steeped in history. Tracing its development back to Paleolithic times, some formidable empires have passed through and shaped its destiny. The medieval Hoysala Empire established a strong kingdom throughout the state, and its illustrious achievements are still visible today in the legacy of superb temples at Belur, Halebid and around Mysore. The cultural vestiges are no less impressive, with Karnataka playing an active role in India's music and literary traditions.

Geographically, the state also has many temptations for the visitor. From the verdant hill plantations of the Western Ghats to the dazzling Arabian Coast beaches, which stretch over the 320km (200 miles) of coastline, there is plenty to please the eye as well as the mind.

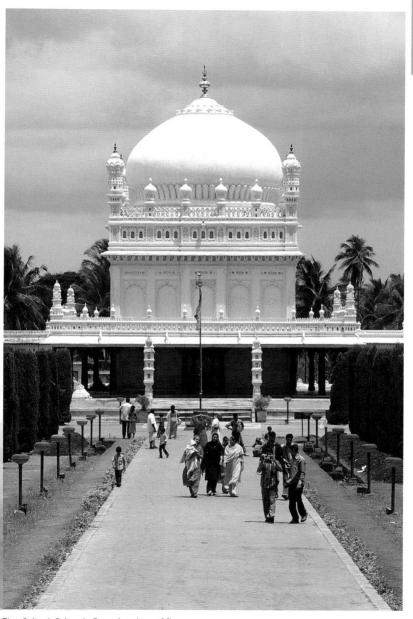

Tipu Sultan's Palace in Bangalore (*see p86*)

BANGALORE
Bangalore city

The capital of Karnataka, Bangalore is known for its strong export and hi-tech industries, making it the capital of India's information technology revolution. Bangalore's industries include electronics, aeronautics, machinery and fashion garments.

While the first impression that most visitors get of Bangalore is of bustling modernity, its tree-lined avenues also justify its title of Garden City, while various monuments testify to a vibrant history.

Bangalore was founded in the 16th century by Kempe Gowda, changing hands frequently. From the mid-18th century, the city was ruled by Hyder Ali, who is credited with the Lalbagh Gardens, which were further developed by his son and successor, Tipu Sultan. Tipu both extended Bangalore and built a wall around it.

After the British overthrew Tipu in 1799, the city began to take on the ordered look of a colonial town, and the process continued over the following century.

Bangalore's airport receives international and domestic flights. It is connected by rail or air to most of the other important cities of Southern India.

Bangalore Palace

This replica of England's Windsor Castle dates from the 1880s and was subsequently sold to the Wodeyar rajas of Mysore, whose descendants still live in it.

Palace Road. Tel: 0802 331 5789/336 0818. Open: daily 10am–6pm. Admission charge.

Bull Temple

One of the earliest monuments of Bangalore, dating from the reign of Kempe Gowda, the Bull Temple is named after the huge monolithic Nandi, the bull of Lord Shiva, which is carved out of stone and decorated with bells. *Basavanagudi. Open: daily 7am–8.30pm. Free admission.*

Cubbon Park

Besides being a welcome green space and having a sports complex, Cubbon Park is of interest to travellers because of its museums. The **Government Museum** here is one of the oldest in Southern India, dating from the 1880s, and it has Neolithic and Harappan relics, fine Hoysala, Chalukya and Chola sculptures, jewellery, textiles, coins, miniature paintings of the Deccani and other schools, and geological exhibits. The **Venkatappa Art Gallery** exhibits the paintings and sculpture of the 20th-century artist after whom it is named, as well as other permanent and temporary exhibitions. The **Visvesvaraya Industrial and Technological Museum** has a good transport collection and informative sections for children. *City Centre. Government Museum/ Venkatappa Art Gallery. Tel: 0802 286 4483. Open: Tue–Sun 10am–5pm. Nominal admission charge (same ticket valid for museum also).*

*Visvesvaraya Industrial and
Technological Museum.
Tel: 0802 286 4009. Open: Mon–Sat
10am–6pm. Admission charge.*

ISKCON Temple

This temple was built by the
International Society for Krishna
Consciousness from 1990 to 1997,
blending the traditional architectural
style of Karnataka with modern
innovation.
*Harikrishna Hill, west of Chord Road.
Tel: 0802 347 1956. Open: daily
7am–1pm & 4–8.30pm.*

Lalbagh Botanical Gardens

Lalbagh was laid out in the mid-1700s
by Sultan Hyder Ali and his son, Tipu,
who were inspired by the Mughal
Gardens of Northern India and the
French gardens of colonies like
Pondicherry. Some of the original trees
that were planted by the Sultans, as well
as by the British (who brought in
gardeners from Kew), still stand. Besides
the exotic plants and trees that can be
seen along the pathway, notable features
of Lalbagh are the Rose Garden, the
Floral Clock and the Glasshouse, which
was inspired by London's Crystal Palace
and holds flower shows on Republic
Day (26 January) and Independence Day
(15 August).
*South of the city centre. Tel: 0802 657
9231. Open: 5.30am–7.30pm. Nominal
admission charge.*

Vidhan Soudha

One of India's most attractive state
secretariat buildings, Vidhan Soudha
was built in the 1950s and has an
impressive granite façade with carved
ledges, huge columns and a dome
crowned by the national emblem.
Nearby are a number of colonial
buildings, including the High Court
of Karnataka.
*Northern edge of Cubbon Park. Closed to
the public.*

ISKCON Temple

Walk: Bangalore's historic centre

When Kempe Gowda founded Bangalore he built a mud fort at the site and mapped out the potential extent with four watchtowers at each corner. While Bangalore's urban sprawl has far exceeded his expectations, the fort still stands. This walk explores the old city centre of Bangalore.

Allow 3 hours to see the monuments.

Start from Tipu Sultan's Palace. The walk covers a short but congested stretch of road.

1 Tipu Sultan's Palace

This palace was started by Sultan Hyder Ali, who was de facto ruler of the city from 1759. His son Tipu then made it his summer palace and extended it in the 1780s and 1790s. Built along the lines of their Daria Daulat Bagh at Srirangapatnam (*pp90–91*), Tipu Sultan called it *Rashk-e-Jannat*, the abode of happiness, envy of heaven. Unusually, the entire structure is built from wood. Though it is no longer in the best of conditions, it is still a hauntingly atmospheric place and has a well-kept garden, wooden walls and ceilings with murals in brilliant colours, cusped arches and teakwood columns with elephant-headed cornices, European-style bases and capitals in brilliant colours. The palace was converted by the British into the Secretariat for Bangalore and now houses a gallery of historical pictures.

Open: daily 8.30am–5.30pm.
Admission charge.
Turn right out of the palace to visit the neighbouring Venkataramanaswamy Temple.

2 Venkataramanaswamy Temple

This temple, built in the Dravidian style with towering *gopuram* gateways, pyramidal towering roof and lavishly carved columns, is reputed to be 300 years old, but it was in fact rebuilt by the Wodeyars, probably sometime during the 18th century.
Open: daily 8.30am–6pm. Closed every other Sat.
At the junction outside the temple, turn left on Krishna Rajendra Road for the Bangalore fort.

3 Bangalore Fort

This 16th-century fort, originally built out of mud by Kempe Gowda, was subsequently fortified by Hyder Ali with stone walls and a moat. The fort today is rather dilapidated and some of the walls

have been damaged, but the impressive granite Delhi Gate and the walls which bear inscriptions give an indication of the military traditions of the period. A plaque marks the spot where the British army breached the walls in 1791. Inside are dungeons, cells and passages.
Bangalore Fort. Tel: 0802 336 0818.
Open: Mon–Sat 10am–6pm.
Admission charge.
Return to the road and continue to the City Market.

4 City Market

This crowded market is one of the busiest places in Bangalore and has a congested bus station. The bazaars, selling all manner of spices, fruits, vegetables and other commodities, are dominated by the impressive domes and minarets of the surrounding mosques.
Open: daily 5am–10pm.
From City Market, retrace your steps to Tipu Sultan's Palace.

Walk: Bangalore's historic centre

MYSORE
Mysore city

Known for its palaces, flower markets, silk textiles and sandalwood factory, Mysore takes its name from the demon, Mahishasura, who, according to legend, was slain on Chamundi Hill overlooking the city by the goddess Chamundeswari.

Karnataka's second-largest city is a microcosm of much of what makes Southern India such a fascinating travel destination. Having served as the headquarters for the Wodeyar royal dynasty, which ruled for over half a century up until Indian independence, Mysore was the capital of the kingdom of the same name. It is the astonishing architectural inheritance of this noble period that today is the jewel in Mysore's crown.

The ostentation of the palaces is offset by another quintessentially Mysorean image – the flower market. In fact, lively markets in general are a characteristic of the city. The town is a trade hub for the silk, sandalwood and incense produced in the region. Mysore is also a good centre for those other Indian staples, yoga and Ayurveda. Both are suited to the town's leisurely, relaxed ambience.

If you're in the area in September or October, the Mysore Dasara, a vibrant ten-day festival dating back to the 15th century, is well worth seeing. Its crux is the procession, which starts from the City Palace, when dancers and musicians parade with elaborately decorated elephants, horses and camels in a riot of colour and commotion. *Mysore is about three hours south of Bangalore by train or road.*

Chamundi Hill

This hill is topped by a temple to Chamundeswari, who is said to have destroyed Mahishasura at this site, and who was a patron deity. *Tel: 0821 259 0027. Open: daily 7am–2pm & 3.30–9pm.*

City Palace

One of the largest palaces in India, Mysore's City Palace was built in 1912 on the site of an earlier wooden palace that was destroyed by fire. The architect, Henry Irwin, blended Hindu, Islamic and European styles. The car passage, complete with cannons and carriages, leads to the doll's pavilion with its sculptures, ceremonial objects, wooden elephant howdah decorated with gold, and antique dolls. The Kalyan Mandap, or wedding hall, has murals recording Dasara and other ceremonial processions, together with gold-painted cast-iron pillars rising to a stained-glass dome painted with peacocks and floral patterns, a massive brass chandelier and mosaic floors.

A marble staircase leads to the Durbar Hall, which has a marble floor inlaid with semi-precious stones and paintings by some of India's greatest artists. The private hall has gold-leaf work on the columns, ivory-inlaid doors, and fine woodwork on the ceiling. A museum in the palace complex exhibits Mysore paintings and relics of Karnataka's princely past. *Mirza Road. Tel: 0821 242 1051. www.mysorepalace.in. Open: daily 10am–5.30pm. Admission charge.*

Jagan Mohan Palace

This palace, built in 1861, was converted by HH Sir Jaya Chama Rajendra into an art gallery in 1955. The galleries display decorative arts, with fine collections of porcelain, glassware and ivory artefacts, as well as portraits of the Mysore royals and British dignitaries, oil paintings and watercolours by Indian artists from the early and mid-20th century, musical instruments and other exhibits.

At the western end of the City Palace. Tel: 0821 242 3693. Open: daily 8.30am–5pm. Admission charge.

Railway Museum

Among its collection, this museum has a vintage steam-driven fire engine, a 1914 MG car that could run on rails, a 1922 narrow-gauge train, a 1920 E-class engine and a 1910 Lever Frame inspection car. Of particular interest is the Sri Ranga Pavilion, which houses an 1899 saloon carriage and its accompanying dining car that once belonged to the Maharaja of Mysore. *Krishnaraja Sagar Road. Open: Tue–Sun 9.30am–6.30pm. Admission charge.*

Mysore's ornate City Palace

Tour: Around Mysore

Mysore makes a good base for a tour of sites of both historic and natural importance. This tour takes in one of Karnataka's most popular bird sanctuaries, one of India's best-known gardens and one of Karnataka's most important forts. Taxis can be hired in Mysore for the tour.

Allow about 6 hours, including sightseeing time.

Take the Bangalore highway to Srirangapatnam, about 12km (7½ miles) north of Mysore.

1 Srirangapatnam

This is an island on the River Kaveri. Its name is derived from the Sri Rangananathaswamy Temple, which was built by a governor of the Ganga kingdom in the 9th century and also served as a refuge for Ramanuja, a religious reformer of the 12th century. Over the years Srirangapatnam played a significant role in the political development of Karnataka, until it was eclipsed by Mysore and Bangalore.

The fort was built in the 15th century by the Vijayanagara rulers, and then became part of the Wodeyar kingdom. It was the headquarters of Hyder Ali, after he ousted the Wodeyars from the area, and it has close associations with Tipu Sultan, who developed the area by introducing agricultural reforms. He was killed in the battle of Srirangapatnam, a battle that helped

Colonel Arthur Wellesley, the future Duke of Wellington, make his military reputation. The fort became a British headquarters with Wellesley as the governor.

The ruins of the triple-walled fort can be seen, including gates, ramparts, dungeons, and cemeteries with British and French gravestones (*Admission free*). There are Hindu temples in the complex, as well as the mosque of Tipu Sultan with its delicately decorated slender minarets and inscriptions.

About 1km (½ mile) east of the fort complex is **Daria Daulat Bagh**, the Garden of the Wealth of the Seas, with its formal gardens surrounding a palace made of teak in an Indo-Saracenic style. The palace has large murals recording the life of Tipu Sultan, especially battle scenes, ornamental arches, gilded paintings and floral decorations on its wooden walls and ceilings, while a museum upstairs exhibits coins, European paintings, manuscripts, engravings and the sultan's belongings.

Sri Rangananathaswamy Temple.
Open: daily 7.30am–1pm & 4–8pm.
Daria Daulat Bagh. Tel: 0823 625 2023.
Open: Sat–Thur 9am–5pm.
Head west for Ranganathittu Bird
Sanctuary, about 3km (2 miles)
upstream from Srirangapatnam.

2 Ranganathittu Bird Sanctuary

One of the country's oldest protected
bird areas, this river site was established
by the Maharaja of Mysore at the
suggestion of India's well-known
ornithologist, Salin Ali, who realised that
a weir created by the Wodeyars in the
17th century had created a reservoir that
was an important habitat for waterfowl.
Today, it is protected by the government
as a bird sanctuary. Boats can be hired at
a jetty for a tour of the islands, where
opportunities abound for getting
remarkably close views of spectacular
congregations of many species, such as
storks, egrets, ibises, cormorants, herons
and plovers, which all breed here.
Crocodiles often bask on the islands, and
some visitors have also seen mongooses,
bonnet macaques and monitor lizards
along the shores. Large roosts of flying
foxes and other bats can also be seen.
Tel: 0821 248 1159. Open: daily
8.30am–6pm. Admission charge.
Drive for about 10km (6¼ miles) west
and then north to Brindavan Gardens.

3 Brindavan Gardens

These gardens are situated by the side
of a reservoir named after Maharaja
Krishnaraj Wodeyar, who built a rock
dam to provide water for the nearby
power station. Large crowds come to
see the fountains and the gardens
which are usually illuminated after
sunset, making an attractive sight.
Tel: 0823 625 7247. Open: daily
8am–8.30pm. Admission charge.
From the gardens, it is a 19km (12-mile)
drive southwards to Mysore.

BELUR AND HALEBID

The Hoysala dynasty ruled southern Karnataka from the 11th to the 13th centuries, and built great temples at Belur and Halebid during the 12th century. The distinctive feature of these temples is that they look modest and squat from a distance but are in fact carved in great detail, with hardly any area of the surface left without ornamentation.

The temples are built out of soft soapstone, making it possible to create deep relief carvings. The star-shaped plan is followed by the base and the shrine, with the high plinth providing a circumambulatory walk for pilgrims. Inside the temples are lathe-turned pillars that resemble the rounded wooden columns found elsewhere, while a bell-shaped tower and exquisite carvings are some of the highlights, blending the Dravidian and northern Nagara styles of architecture. The sculpture is magnificently detailed. *Hassan is the nearest railway station to Halebid and Belur. There are hotels in and around Hassan.*

Belur

Once the capital of the Hoysala kingdom, Belur is home to the 12th-century **Chennakesava Temple** (*Open: daily sunrise–sunset. Free admission*), built by King Vishnuvardhana. The temple – which is still very much in use – is set in a courtyard, along with a number of smaller shrines, and its exterior displays some exquisite sculptures of female figures, bands of elephants, musicians, dancers and deities, and perforated screens carved with tales from the *Puranas*. Inside, the Narsimha column has astonishing detail, while the sanctum contains a sculpture of Krishna with his consorts.

Halebid

The **Hoysaleshwara Temple** at Halebid (*Open: daily sunrise–sunset. Free admission*) is the largest of the Hoysala temples, even though it is unfinished. It has the usual star-shaped plinth, complete with bands of elephants, lions and horsemen, floral scrolls and outstanding narrative friezes with scenes from the Hindu epics. The temple is carved with fine images of Brahma on his swan, Krishna playing a flute, and Ravana trying to shake Mount Kailasha, the abode of Lord Shiva. The lawns of the temple are very attractive and display a museum of sculptures.

A short distance from the Hoysala temple, some Jain shrines exhibit lathe-turned columns.

Sravanabelagola

Most visitors to the temples of Halebid and Belur also visit Sravanabelagola to see the colossal statue of Gomateshwara that is sacred to Jains (*Open: daily sunrise–sunset*). One of India's largest freestanding sculptures, the 10th-century statue, about 17m (56ft) high, is reached by a flight of about 700 steps after a strenuous climb. The nude statue has elongated arms and wide shoulders that are somewhat out of proportion, but the hands, hair and serene face are perfectly carved. The statue tells of Bahubali, who defeated his elder brother Bharat over a right of succession, but, after winning the battle, realised its futility and adopted a life of meditation and asceticism. The depth of his meditation is depicted with creeper growing on his limbs and anthills and snakes at his feet.

The ascent to the statue leads past Jain shrines, most of them dating from the 12th century, and some have very fine carvings. There are also Jain temples in the town and on nearby Chandragiri Hill. *Buses run to Sravanabelagola from Channarayapatha, 10km (6¼ miles) to the northwest.*

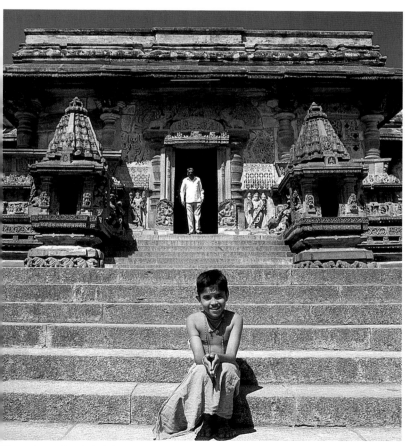

Chennakesava Temple in Belur

KODAGU

With its forests, waterfalls and plantations, Kodagu district, often called the Coorg region, is one of the most scenically attractive areas of Karnataka. Once ruled by regional kings, the Haleri rajas, Kodagu has a distinct cultural identity that differs from that of the rest of Karnataka, with its own cuisine, language and costumes, along with a strong pride in its martial tradition.

Markets called *shantes* are held weekly and can be experienced on Fridays at Madikeri and at Kushalnagar. Among the many attractions of the area are Sidhapur, which is one of the major coffee-growing areas, the Dubare forests and elephant camp, and Kakkabe, which makes a good starting point for climbing Thadiyandamol, at 1,750m (5,741ft) the highest peak in the region. The island of Nisargadhama, on the River Kaveri near Kushalnagar, is a good spot for birdwatching, amid a pleasant setting of parkland and a variety of trees, including bamboo and sandalwood.

Bylakuppe

A number of Tibetan settlements are scattered around Bylakuppe, which is one of the largest areas of Tibetan Buddhism in Southern India. Here Buddhists have established craft cooperatives as well as schools. One of the most important monasteries here is the *gompa* at Sera which serves as the

Mahayana Buddhist University, one of India's foremost learning centres for Tibetan monks or lamas. The most prominent feature of the *gompa* is the massive image of Shakyamuni Buddha. Another of the region's attractions is the **Golden Temple of Namdroling**, a beautifully painted monastery in peaceful grounds. The prayer hall has enormous gilt statues of Guru Padmasambava, Shakyamuni Buddha and Buddha Amitayus, richly decorated columns with dragon motifs, *thangka* wall paintings, a beautiful casket, and galleries that offer an insight into Tantric Buddhism. Another important monastery in the region is at **Tashi Lhunpo**.
Bylakuppe and the monasteries can be accessed from the Mysore–Madikeri Highway.
Mahayana Buddhist University. Tel: 0822 325 8435. www.serajeymonastery.org.
Golden Temple. Tel: 0822 325 4036. www.palyul.org. Open: 7am–8pm.
Tashi Lhunpo Monastery. www.tashilhunpo.org. Permit required well in advance to visit.

Madikeri

The market town of Madikeri, which is the capital of Kodagu district, spreads along the edges of the hills. The town's main attractions are the 19th-century **Omkareshwar Temple**, which exhibits a fascinating blend of Kerala-style pagoda roofing and façades with Islamic domes. Near the temple is a fort with stone gateways, while

t Mark's Church, within the
ortifications, is now a museum
howing British relics, Jain and Hindu
culpture, and regional art and culture.
Nearby are the royal cenotaphs and an
8th-century Shiva Temple. **Raja's Seat**,
aid to have been a royal pavilion, has a
uperb view of the surrounding hilly
ountryside.

An uphill road through coffee estates
nd woods leads to the Abbi Falls
vhich are set among pepper and
lowering vines, cardamom plants,
amboos and forested hillsides.
Madikeri is about three hours by road
rom Mysore.
Omkareshwar Temple. Open: daily
.30am–noon & 5–8pm.
t Mark's Church Museum.

Open: Tue–Sun 10am–5.30pm.
Free admission.
Raja's Seat. Open: daily 5.30am–7.30pm.

Talakaveri

Spelt Talacauveri on some maps, this is
considered to be a source of the River
Kaveri and is therefore a place of
pilgrimage for Hindus. In October,
during a festival called Kaveri
Sankaramana, pilgrims come to bathe in
the river and to visit the springs. About
8km (5 miles) away, at Bhagamandala,
is the Triveni bathing *ghat* at the
confluence of the Kaveri, Kanike and
Suiyorhi rivers. The Bhandeshwara
Temple here is a striking Kerala-style
building in a large stone courtyard.
48km (30 miles) west of Madikeri.

he stunning Kodagu landscape

Karnataka

HISTORIC TOWNS OF NORTHERN KARNATAKA

Northern Karnataka comprises the northern part of the Deccan Plateau, and it is veined by the Tungabhadra, Krishna, Doni and Gataprabha rivers.

Some of the area's main attractions are the great temples established by the Chalukya rulers in the 6th and 7th centuries. These include those at the World Heritage Site of Pattadakal, the Vijayanagara temples and courtly architecture of the 14th to 16th centuries at Hampi, which is also a World Heritage Site, and the 15th- to 17th-century mosques and mausoleum complexes of Bijapur and Bidar, which are regarded as some of the best examples of Islamic architecture in Southern India.

Aihole

Generally referred to as the cradle of temple architecture, Aihole has more than 100 temples built in different styles including the early Chalukyan, late Chalukyan, Hoysala, Nagara and Dravidian from the 6th to the 12th centuries. The best known is the Durgigudi or Durga Temple, so-named because of its location near the 'Durg' or fort walls, and noted for its early *gopuram*-style entrance structure, Buddhist-style semicircular apse, and elevated plinths featuring panels of intricate carvings. The gallery around the sanctum displays a series of elaborate sculptures in niches; these include Lord Shiva with Nandi, Narasimha, Lord Vishnu with Garuda,

Varaha or the boar incarnation of Lord Vishnu, Durga or Chamundi destroying the buffalo-headed demon Mahishasura, and Harihara, the combination of Vishnu and Shiva. Amorous couples are sculpted on the columns, and the entrance doorway to the hall has outstandingly fine sculpture.

46km (29 miles) northeast of Badami.
110km (68 miles) south of Bijapur.
Durga Temple. Tel: 0835 128 4533.
Open: daily 8am–6pm.
Admission charge.

Badami

Badami was the stronghold of the Chalukya rulers, who excavated caves in the sandstone cliffs around the town and built impressive temples at Aihole and Pattadakal.

Badami has a railway station. There are hotels and places to eat in the town.

Badami cave temples

The caves cut into the sandstone ridges of Badami in the 6th and 7th centuries are said to have influenced the design of structural temples built later on in the Deccan. The four cave temples, three Hindu and one Jain, are known for their fine sculptural work, including the minute detail of the jewellery worn by the deities and the smaller figures. Cave 3, which is dedicated to Vishnu, is generally considered to be the most impressive of the four, not only because of its elaborate sculptural decoration but also because of its sheer size. The cave has striking depictions of couples

as carved brackets, Lord Vishnu on the coils of the serpent Anantha, and Vishnu's incarnations as Narasimha, the man-lion combination that disembowelled a demon, and Varah or the boar incarnation. The sculpted columns and fine images of Indra on an elephant, Shiva on a bull and Brahma riding a swan on the ceiling panels are among the most detailed in Badami.
Open: daily sunrise–sunset. Admission charge.

Bidar

At the centre of Bidar is the medieval walled town of the Sultans, with its many mosques, a great 15th-century *madrasa* or theological college with a towering minaret and fine mosaics, and a fort built by the Chalukyas and strengthened during the reign of the Sultans after Ahmed Shah made the town his capital in the 15th century. The fort contains the remains of palaces, such as the Rangin Mahal, with its fine woodcarvings and inlay work. Ashtur, east of Bidar, has some impressive domed mausoleums of the Sultans.
137km (85 miles) northwest of Hyderabad.
Madrasa. Open: daily sunrise–sunset. Free admission.
Fort. Open: daily sunrise–sunset. Free admission.
Mausoleums. Open: daily sunrise–sunset. Free admission.

Bijapur

Bijapur's building boom came in the 16th and 17th centuries after the five Islamic rulers of the Deccan joined forces to invade the Vijayanagara capital of Hampi.

The town's largest and most celebrated monument, the **Golgumbaz**, was built as the mausoleum of Muhammad Adil Shah in the 17th century. The hallway of the main mausoleum is one of the largest in the world to be covered by a single hemispherical dome, which also dominates the townscape. The **Ibrahim Rauza**, one of the highlights of Bijapuri

Golgumbaz mausoleum, Bijapur

architecture, was built by Ibrahim II, who came to the throne in the 1580s, and his wife, Taj Sultana. The mausoleum has minarets, cupolas, stone filigree, fine sculptural work, pierced windows and decorative panels. It also exhibits elaborate Koranic inscriptions that rank among the best in India. Bijapur's Juma Masjid, or **Jami Masjid**, dating from the 16th century, is one of the Deccan's finest mosques. Superbly proportioned and topped by onion domes, the mosque has an arcaded court with a square tank. The court leads to the main prayer hall, with its elegant central dome surrounded by 33 smaller domes. The *mihrab* or prayer niche is richly embellished with gold work, calligraphy and floral decorations.

Bijapur has a railway station and a few hotels. Golgumbaz. Tel: 0835 224 0737. Open: daily 6am–6pm. Admission charge. Ibrahim Rauza. Open: daily 6am–5.40pm. Admission charge. Jami Masjid. Open: daily 9am–5.30pm. Free admission.

Hampi

Hampi epitomises the grandeur of the great Vijayanagara Empire, which is regarded as the largest Hindu empire of Southern India. The town is home to clusters of ruined monuments, called the **Royal Centre** and the **Sacred Centre**, and scores of temples and other buildings set among the hills and along the Tungabhadra River. The most glorious period of Hampi was during the reign of Krishnadevraya, who saw

the Vijayanagara Empire grow in power, wealth and extent. Great patrons of art, the Vijayanagara rulers also worked towards the development of agriculture, textiles and new technologies.

Hampi is near Hospet, a town with a railway station and a few hotels.

Royal Centre

The best representation of the courtly style of the Vijayanagara dynasty, which drew on both Hindu and Islamic architectural styles, is the 16th-century **Lotus Mahal**, screened by a wall as it was probably built for the queens (though some believe it was a council chamber as the elephant stables are nearby), with cusped arches, bracketed windows and pyramidal domes. The **elephant stables** have ten domed chambers, with vaulted entrances representing different architectural styles, and beams to which elephants could be chained, around a central pavilion, with a guardhouse at the entrance.

The hydraulic engineering skills of the Vijayanagara rulers can be seen in the tanks, ducts, canals and sluices that carried water to different areas.

3km (2 miles) south of Hampi. Lotus Mahal & elephant stables. Open: daily 8am–5.30pm. Admission charge (one ticket covers same-day entry to various attractions).

Sacred Centre

Some of the temples of Hampi predate the Vijayanagara kingdom. The oldest is probably the **Virupaksha Temple**, still

in use today, which has *gopuram* gatehouses added by the Vijayanagara rulers, as well as some of the few remaining examples of the Vijayanagara style of painting. A short walk from the Virupaksha Temple, the **Vithala Temple** is considered to be one of the finest examples of Vijayanagara architecture. Believed to date from the 16th century, the temple contains the famous 'Hampi chariot', a shrine designed in the shape of a wooden chariot on wheels, with fine carvings including a depiction of Garuda, the eagle mount of Lord Vishnu. The open *mandapa* or hallway features intricate carvings, while the slender, superbly carved columns produce musical notes when struck. The ceiling is beautifully carved with floral and geometric patterns. The other columned halls also have interesting carvings.
Virupaksha Temple. Open: daily 6am–8pm (closes for 2 hours around noon). Vithala Temple. Open: daily 8am–5.30pm.

Pattadakal

Once the site of coronation ceremonies of the Chalukyan rulers, Pattadakal's temples date from the 3rd to the 7th centuries and are considered to represent the most mature phase of Western Chalukya architecture. Some of the temples were built by the Rashtrakutas after they took over the kingdom from the Chalukya dynasty. The best known are the **Malikarjuna** and **Virupaksha** temples, which were built for two sisters, who were queens of the Chalukyan ruler, Vikramaditya. They have richly carved three-storey towers, with striking panels showing different forms of Shiva and Vishnu, and a carved base. Like most of the temples of Southern India, the interiors are also exquisitely carved, with the pillars of the Virupaksha Temple relating tales from the *Ramayana* and *Mahabharata* epics, while those of the Malikarjuna Temple are carved in delicately executed relief and depict scenes from the life of Krishna. Other carvings in the temples reflect the courtly and social life of the Chalukyas.
17km (10½ miles) from Aihole. Temples. Open: daily 6am–6pm. Admission charge.

Virupaksha Temple, Hampi

Tamil Nadu

In a country that frequently throws up stark juxtapositions of old and new, Tamil Nadu offers a noteworthy microcosm. Along with some of the most antediluvian roots, such as the three-and-a-half-millennia-old Tamil civilisation, the state is also India's most urbanised one, exemplified by the industrial and cultural engine of its capital, Chennai. A diverse topography, from semi-arid inland regions to mountains to fine beaches and lagoons, provides further reason to spend time in this rewarding state.

Tamil Nadu ('Country of the Tamils') extends from India's southernmost point up the country's eastern coast and far inland. Bordering Kerala to the west, Karnataka to the northwest and Andhra Pradesh to the north, its coastline adjoins the world's largest bay, the Bay of Bengal. It also contains the enclave of Puducherry, better known as Pondicherry, the largest region of the union territory of the same name, a former French colony.

Tamil Nadu's landscape boasts enormous variety. There are mountains – this is the only state to include part of both the Western and the Eastern Ghats, along with their meeting point of the Nilgiri Hills. The forests of the latter are rich in wildlife, in particular of the avian and elephantine kind. Waterfowl and wading birds can also be spotted in the coastal wetlands and the Gulf of Mannar. Some elevated parts of Tamil Nadu also yield a lush plant life.

A generous coastline of over 900km (560 miles) gives the state some fabulous stretches of sand (including one of the longest beaches in Asia), and these are increasingly popular with tourists. But history is probably the big deal in Tamil Nadu. The coast is home to a chain of Dravidian Temples, pyramidal constructions that date back several millennia. It may be a cliché, but the past truly comes alive in this part of India. The Tamil civilisation is a living classical civilisation whose language, literature, art and architecture have thrived since ancient times. Part of the pleasure of visiting – to history buffs, at least – is immersion in a culture that retains vestiges of a time preceding the Common Era.

All of which is not to say that Tamil Nadu is stuck in the past. One of India's most developed states, it has a thriving economic engine and is firmly hitched to India's IT bandwagon. Capital Chennai is one of the country's four biggest cities, and its British buildings, along with the French influence that permeates Pondicherry, give Tamil Nadu a truly international flavour.

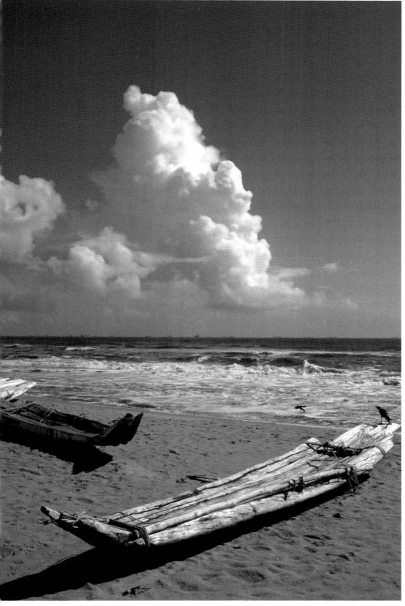

The Indian Ocean near Chennai

CHENNAI
Chennai city

Chennai, or Madras, is the capital of Tamil Nadu, and it is often considered to be the gateway to Southern India as it has the largest international airport among the four states. One of the four metropolises of India, it is also an important port and industrial centre.

The city is a relatively modern one, established by the British in the 17th century, but incorporating ancient sites and old Portuguese villages. Because the British stayed here longer than in other cities of Southern India, Chennai has some of India's earliest and most impressive examples of colonial architecture.

330km (205 miles) east of Bangalore, Chennai has an international airport.

Churches

It is believed that Thomas the Apostle arrived in Kerala and took refuge in the Little Mount Caves south of Chennai. The **Basilica of San Thome** is one of the city's famous churches; it was probably founded in the 16th century, and is situated in an area that used to be a Portuguese enclave. The present cathedral dates from the 1890s, and was built in the Gothic style. St Thomas Mount in the cantonment is associated with the last years of St Thomas, and it has a 16th-century church.

Basilica. Tel: 0442 498 5455. www.santhomechurch.com. Open: daily 5am–9pm. Free admission.

Egmore

Egmore is home to some of Chennai's best-known colonial buildings, including **St Andrew's Kirk**, built in the 1820s. This church is a fine example of the architecture of this period, with its towering steeple, columned nave and huge dome, painted with stars on a blue background and supported by Corinthian columns. The Egmore Railway Station and the municipal buildings and colleges are other important colonial structures here.

St Andrew's Kirk, Poonamallee High Rd. Tel: 0442 561 2608. www.standrewskirk.org. Open: daily 8am–6pm. Free admission.

Government Museum

This museum is one of the best and most comprehensive in Southern India. Established in the mid-19th century, it is a red circular building with Mughal influences and European columns housing a museum and a theatre, as well as the **National Art Gallery**, which was designed by Henry Irwin in the early 20th century and is situated in the same compound. The museum's collections include tools, jewellery and weapons from the Stone and Iron ages. One of the most important collections is of sculpture, especially those found at Amrawati and other Buddhist sites of Andhra, such as Nagarjunakonda and Goli. They include relief panels telling the life of Buddha, images of the *Jataka* tales, a votive slab from the Amrawati *stupa*, and statues of Buddha. There are also impressive stone sculptures from Tamil Nadu and Karnataka which represent Pallava, Chola, Hoysala and Chalukyan art.

The museum is also well known for its bronze gallery. Its superb collection of 9th- to 13th-century metal sculpture, ranging from about 4cm (1½ in) to over 1m (3ft) tall, is significant, as Tamil Nadu was known for its bronze-casting industry. The collections include numerous Chola sculptures of Natraja, which symbolise the motion and power of Shiva's cosmic dance in detail,

Somaskadas showing seated Shiva and Parvati with or without Skanda their son, Shiva in meditation sculptured in great detail, Ardhanaishvara, and the renowned figures of the *Ramayana* from Thanjavur.

The ethnology gallery has clothes, weapons and photographs of tribal groups, and a remarkable collection of musical instruments.
Government Museum, 406 Pantheon Rd, Egmore. Tel: 0442 819 3238.
www.chennaimuseum.org.
Open: Sat–Thur 9.30am–5pm (last admission 4.30pm). Admission charge.

Tamil Nadu

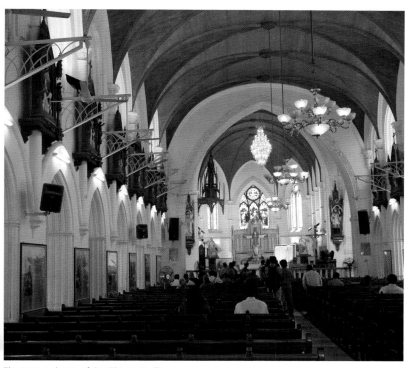

The nave and apse of San Thome Basilica

Walk: Fort George

Fort George marks the foundation of Madras, today's Chennai. Constructed in the mid-17th century, much of the fort today consists of more recent structures, built after damage incurred from French and other attacks. The thick walls still stand and some of Chennai's grandest colonial buildings can be seen in this area.

Allow 3 hours to see the fort and its neighbouring buildings.

Start at St Mary's Church.

1 St Mary's Church

St Mary's Church is one of the oldest Anglican churches in Asia. It was built in the 1680s and renovated in the 18th century. With its thick walls and strong roof designed to withstand cannonballs, the church was used as a storehouse and safe refuge during sieges. The interior is filled with plaques, paintings and statues, many of them depicting key figures in the history of British India, including the former governor of Chennai, Elihu Yale, after whom the famous university is named.

Robert Clive – Clive of India – married his wife Margaret here, and Job Charnock, founder of Kolkata, is believed to have had his daughters baptised here. The church also has some interesting tombstones.
Tel: 0442 567 0389. Admission charge. Open: daily 9am–5pm.
A short walk from the church is the Fort Museum.

2 Fort Museum

The Fort Museum occupies three floors of the imposing 18th-century Fort House, which was the main bank and exchange during the colonial period. The museum narrates the history of the British occupation of Chennai, with palanquins, padlocks, flags, weapons, East India Company coins, medals and stamps, as well as uniforms, and fascinating letters written by Clive and Cornwallis. The art gallery here has portraits, oil paintings and sketches.
Tel: 0442 567 0389. Open: Sat–Thur 10am–5pm. Admission charge.
From the Fort Museum, continue along the busy main road to the High Court.

3 The High Court

This judicial building is a splendid example of the kind of Indo-Saracenic architecture promoted by architects such as Henry Irwin. It is a magnificent red building with bulbous white domes, sandstone minarets and spires, and a tall central tower that is a prominent

landmark of the city. The interiors of the High Court are equally attractive, with a profusion of stained glass, woodwork, silver panels and ceiling paintings. Nearby is the equally opulent Law College campus, with elaborate twin towers.
Tel: 0442 534 0410.
*www.hcmadras.tn.nic.in; hcourt@
tn.nic.in. Open: Mon–Sat 10am–5pm.
Free admission; nominal charge for a
guided tour.*

From the judicial complex it is possible to cross to the grid of streets of George Town. This area has historic temples such as Chennakesava and Kalikambal, an Armenian Church, an Indo-Saracenic building (now the State Bank of India), the robust red General Post Office designed by Robert Chisholm and completed in the 1880s (ask for GPO), and Bentinck's Building, built in Regency style. However, do bear in mind that this is a chaotic, congested and rather unkempt area.

Tour: Artists' villages

The East Coast road from Chennai to Mahabalipuram (Mamallapuram) passes some of the most important arts and crafts complexes in Tamil Nadu.

From Chennai to Mahabalipuram is 58km (36 miles). Allow around three hours.

Take the road 18km (11 miles) south from central Chennai to Injambakkan to see the Cholamandal Artists' Village.

1 Cholamandal Artists' Village

Established in 1966 to promote the development of contemporary art in India, this village is a place where artists live, work and exhibit their paintings and sculpture. Today, there are many studios and galleries in traditionally designed buildings where paintings, sketches, sculpture, metalwork and other arts are exhibited, and pieces can be bought by visitors. It is sometimes possible to see artists at work in the village or at the galleries. In 2009, the Cholamandal Centre for Contemporary Art was opened at the village. This new two-storey building houses a permanent collection and a commercial gallery.
Tel: 0442 449 0092. cholaartist.co.in.
Open: daily 10am–5pm.
About 12km (7$\frac{1}{2}$ miles) south of Cholamandal Artists' Village, the highway brings you to Dakshin Chitra.

2 Dakshin Chitra

This heritage centre is one of India's best folk museums, and it encapsulates the culture and crafts of the four states of Southern India. Set up by a crafts

Stonemason at Dakshin Chitra

foundation in Chennai, it subsequently received government and international support. In the reception area there is an audiovisual presentation introducing visitors to the concept of the centre and the culture of the states represented. From here, visitors enter an open-air display of domestic architecture from the 19th and 20th centuries, some of which are original buildings that have been relocated to this site. On show are the village huts, houses and workshops of weavers, potters and other artisans, the homes of Tamil Brahmins and merchants, majestic Chettinad mansions containing Chinese crafts and Burmese teak furniture, the wooden Syrian Christian houses of central Kerala, and the Nair mansions of northern Kerala. The complex has successfully re-created an authentic atmosphere of Southern India's dwellings from all four states.

Exhibitions express the cultural diversity of Southern India through textiles such as silk and cotton dresses from different communities, along with various arts and crafts. They also provide information on the traditions of puppetry, dance and tribal cults.

Artisans work on traditional techniques of pottery, basket-weaving, carving, puppet-making, palm leaf decoration and other craftwork. There are also shops and a restaurant.

Music and dance performances are organised here from time to time. *Tel: 0442 747 2603. www.dakshinachitra.net. Open: Wed– Mon 10am–6pm. Admission charge. From Dakshin Chitra, continue south towards Mahabalipuram. To the north of the village is the Government College of Architecture and Sculpture.*

3 Government College of Architecture and Sculpture

This is one of the colleges established by the Government of Tamil Nadu to promote sculpture, architecture, music, dance and other traditions of the state. A non-autonomous college under the University of Madras, this can be a good place to gain an insight into the sculptural work of the region, from the preliminary drawings to the execution. The classical tradition of sculpture has strict rules regarding proportion and Hindu iconography. You can get permission to visit from the college office. *From the college, the road continues to Mahabalipuram. A visit may be made to the Tiger Cave, a rock-cut Durga shrine with elaborate lion-head carvings believed to date from the 7th century. With its superb acoustics, the cave may have once been used for performances.*

MAHABALIPURAM
Mahabalipuram town

Named after Mahabali, the demon destroyed by Vishnu, Mahabalipuram (also known as Mamallapuram) is one of the greatest draws of Tamil Nadu, with its shore temple and other beautifully sculpted monuments, lively sculptural tradition and travellers' enclave. The variety of fine sculpture seen here has given it the status of an open-air art museum as it shows the progression of Dravida architecture from rock-cut caves through the roofed *ratha* shrines to the shore temple.

Mahabalipuram is 58km (36 miles) south of Chennai.

Cave temples

The hillside cave temple complex is architecturally interesting as it demonstrates the early Dravida style. One of the most famous caves is the Krishna Mandapam, showing Lord Krishna protecting his people from the wrath of the rain god Indra by lifting Lord Govardhan as an umbrella. Other scenes show Krishna milking a cow and playing a flute. The Ganesh Mandapam is a living shrine and the Trimurthi temple celebrates the trinity of Vishnu, Brahma and Shiva. The Varaha Mandapam has panels showing two reincarnations of Vishnu, Lakshmi and courtly scenes; it also has a water-storage area which is used by pilgrims. The Mahisuramardini Cave is probably the most remarkable, with its carved panel depicting Durga astride a lion and destroying the demon, Mahishasura. The panel also shows Vishnu reclining on his serpent, and statues of Shiva with his consort and his son, Skanda.

An imposing bas-relief near the *mandapas* shows Arjuna, one of the five Pandava brothers, meditating on a nearby statue of Lord Shiva, and a huge elephant leading a procession.

Rathas

The five *rathas* are monolithic, chariot-like shrines sculpted out of rock in the 7th century, each one architecturally distinct. They demonstrate the evolution of temple architecture in Southern India, with *gopuram*, *mandapa* hall and the sanctum, crowned by pyramidal roofs. The tallest of the *rathas* is the pyramidal domed Dharmaraja Ratha, with its row of pavilions and panels of figures dedicated to Lord Shiva, while the largest is the vaulted Bhima which houses an image of Lord Vishnu. The Draupadi Ratha is unique in having a roof resembling that of a thatched house but made of stone. Near the *rathas* stand a sculpted elephant, a lion and a Nandi, the mounts of Indra, Durga and Shiva.

Shore temple

A world heritage site, this shore temple on the coast of the Bay of Bengal is considered by many to be the climax of Pallava architecture at Mahabalipuram.

Though eroded by wind, salt and sand, the temple is still remarkable for the extent of the detail that remains even today. The temple is fairly compact, with two finely carved towers, the taller of them standing over a cell facing the sea and showing the introduction of the lion pillar which was the hallmark of this kind of architecture. Built in the 7th to 8th centuries by Rajasimha, the temple is unique in having shrines to both Shiva and Vishnu. It is enclosed by a wall which has panels of animal figures.

Rathas *and Shore temple. Open: daily 6.30am–6pm. Joint admission charge.*

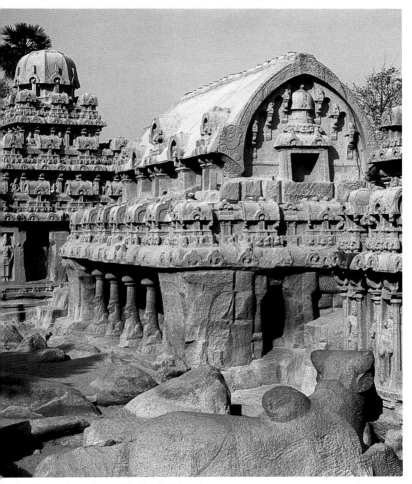

Intricately carved temples, sculpted in the 7th century

KANCHIPURAM
Kanchipuram town

Kanchipuram was the capital of the Pallavas and flourished after their decline. Considered a meeting place for the scholars of three great religions, Hinduism, Buddhism and Jainism, Kanchipuram was a major centre of learning, culture and philosophy, associated with leaders like Sankaracharya and Bodhidharma.

It now houses the remains of Pallava, Chola and Vijayanagara architecture, with its magnificent temples embodying the political importance of Kanchipuram as well as the various stages of architecture from the earlier compact form to the taller *gopurams* and enclosures of the 17th-century temples.

Dubbed the 'golden city of a thousand temples', Kanchipuram is one of the seven holy towns of Hinduism and one of the most important Hindu pilgrim centres of Southern India.

Kanchipuram also has a long history as a weaving centre. For over four centuries it has been famous for its silk sarees with their rich gold thread patterns, and it is also gaining fame for its cotton textiles. Weavers can be watched at work at centres in the town.

As Kanchipuram has more than 70 temples, it is best to aim to visit just a handful over a day or two's stay in the town, or on a day excursion.
Kanchipuram is about 76km (47 miles) west of Chennai.

Ekambaranatha Temple

This is one of the largest of the temples in the town, with five enclosures and a multi-pillared hall called the 1,000-columned *mandapa*. Begun by the Pallavas, the temple developed under the Cholas and was enlarged further by the Vijayanagara rulers who built the high *gopuram* and the outer wall in the 16th century. Dedicated to Lord Shiva, the temple has a tank to its west and an earthen *lingam* to its east. A carved panel tells the tale of its origins.
Puthupalayam Street. Open: daily 6am–12.30pm & 4–8pm. Nominal admission charge. Sanctum closed to non-Hindus.

Kailasanatha Temple

Rated by most visitors as the most beautiful of the town's temples and also thought to be its oldest, dating from the 8th century, this temple was built from sandstone by the Pallavas. The temple is topped by a pyramidal tower and the walls have cell-like shrines, some with frescoes and *Nandis*. The shrines around the sanctum demonstrate the temple's architectural connection to the *rathas* of Mahabalipuram, but Kanchipuram's temple is considered to represent the mature phase of Pallava architecture as it has granite foundations and finer carvings than those of Mahabalipuram.
Putleri Street. Open: daily 6am–12.30pm & 4–8.30pm. Free admission.

Tamil Nadu

Vaikuntha Perumal Temple

Also dedicated to Vishnu, this temple is from the 8th century and is a step up from the older Kailasanatha Temple in its workmanship. Bas-relief panels illustrate battles between Pallavas and Chalukyas, as well as other scenes of courtly life. The lofty tower over the sanctum crowns three shrines. The entrance gateway was added by the Vijayanagara rulers.

Kamakshi Amman Sannathi Street.
Open: daily 5am–12.30pm & 4–8.30pm.
Free admission.

Varadaraja Temple

This temple, dedicated to Vishnu, is one of the most important religious centres for pilgrims to Kanchipuram. Built in the 11th century but enlarged during the Vijayanagara period, the temple has a superbly carved *mandapa*, one of the most exquisite in Tamil Nadu, and its main shrine is built on an elephant-shaped rock.

3km (2 miles) southeast of town.
Open: 7am–noon & 3.30–8pm.
Free admission.
Sanctum closed to non-Hindus.

The beautiful sandstone Kailasanatha Temple

PONDICHERRY
Pondicherry town

The capital of the French colonies in India, Pondicherry was ruled by European colonial powers from the 16th century. The French rule was marked by conflicts with the Dutch and the British who captured the colony for short periods. After 1816, the town began to enjoy peace, and in 1954 Pondicherry was handed over to the Government of India and became a union territory with Kariakal further south, Mahe on the Malabar coast and Yanam in Andhra.

The town retains some of its Gallic flavour in its colonial buildings, and in the French houses of the old quarters. Street signs continue to show both the French and the new Indian names, and the uniforms of the traffic police are still French influenced, while French and Indo-French food is still served in some restaurants.

Aurodhan Art Gallery

The Aurodhan Art Gallery showcases the work of contemporary artists. The exhibits show local influences, including those of the ashrams.
33 rue François Martin.
Tel: 0413 222 2795. www.aurodhan.com; aurodhan@satyam.net.in. Visitors' office open: daily 9am–5.30pm.
Admission charge.

Auroville

The communes of Auroville, inspired by The Mother (an early 20th-century

spiritual leader at the Sri Aurobindo Ashram in Pondicherry), were founded in the 1960s. The place is run on alternative sources of energy, and work here includes handicrafts, organic agriculture and educational projects.
6km (4 miles) north of Pondicherry.
www.auroville.org

Churches

The French influence is visible in the various churches built from the 17th to the 19th centuries, among them the **Church of our Lady of Immaculate Conception**, the **Church of Our Lady of Angels** which has an oil painting given to the church by the king, and the huge **Church of the Sacred Heart of Jesus** which is one of the most impressive, with stained glass and Gothic features.

Goubert Salai

The beachside promenade of Pondicherry offers a glimpse of some of the town's colonial architecture. The **Hotel de Ville** now houses government offices, while a memorial honours Indian soldiers who allied with the French. There is also a French-style square, the Raj Nivas, and a number of other buildings that are relics of French colonial rule.

Government Museum

The Pondicherry Museum displays Neolithic and Roman artefacts, and it has a sculpture gallery with Pallava, Chola, Vijayanagara and Buddhist pieces. It also has a French gallery with furniture and artefacts from the colony, as well as art, handicrafts and geology. There is also a good shell collection. *49 St Louis Street, opp. Government Park. Tel: 0413 233 6203. Open: Tue–Sun 10am–5pm. Nominal admission charge.*

Sri Aurobindo Ashram

One of India's best-known ashrams, this one was founded in the 1920s by Bengali guru Aurobindo Ghose and The Mother. It continues to be the centre of the society he founded, and has beautifully kept gardens with cacti, a rockery and a flower garden, as well as a Samadhi (memorial) of Aurobindo and The Mother, which is covered with flowers. The centre has a few shops, and opposite the ashram is an international centre which sometimes has various programmes worth finding out about if you are in the area. *Information Centre, 3 Rangapillai St. Tel: 0413 223 3604. www.sriaurobindoashram.com; bureaucentral@sriaurobindoashram.com. Bureau Central open: daily 6am–8pm. Free admission.*

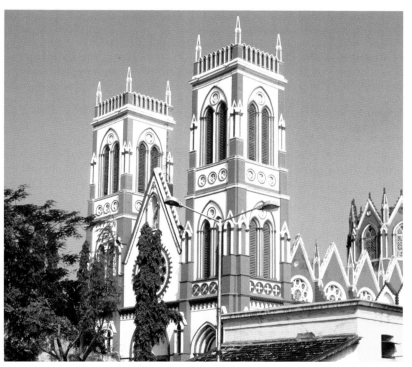

Sacred Heart Church, Pondicherry

CENTRAL TAMIL NADU

The heart of Tamil Nadu, mainly comprising the delta of the Kaveri River, is home to some of the state's most famous temples. This was the stronghold of the Cholas from the 9th to the 13th centuries, and most of the temples in this region were built during their reign, but the Nayakas also contributed to the temple architecture of Thanjavur. Touring this area also gives an insight into the arts of the Tamil rulers, from the superb bronzes and paintings of Thanjavur to the songs of Sangam literature that are still enjoyed today.

Chidambaram

According to legend, Chidambaram is said to be the site of the cosmic dance of Shiva as Natraja who defeated a goddess in a dance competition, ending with the dance of bliss. He is revered here as Natraja, the king of dance, at the **Sabhanayaka Natraja Temple**, which was largely built by the Cholas. Entered through massive *gopuram* gateways, the temple has a gold-plated roof and is noted for its sculpted dance figures depicting the movements of the Natya-Shastra. The centrepiece is the sanctum in the inner enclosure, with its famous Natraja bronzes.

Sabhanayaka Temple, Ayikulam Rd. Open: daily 6am–12.30pm & 4 or 4.30–10.30pm. Free admission. Chidambaram is about six hours south of Chennai by road or rail.

Kumbakonam

A former capital of the Cholas, this town has a large number of impressive temples, including the 13th-century **Sarangapani Temple** which is entered through a tall *gopuram* whose central shrine dates from the Chola period. The temple has intricately carved latticed screens. The 17th-century **Kumbareswara Temple** has a holy *lingam*, while the **Nageshwara Swami Shiva Temple** has fine carvings around the main shrine walls, dating from the 9th to the 10th centuries and rated among the finest in Southern India. The town is important to Hindu devotees, who believe that the Mahmakham tank was the site where the drink of immortality flowed out of Shiva's broken pot and was washed away by holy waters. This town also makes a good base to visit Dasasuram's **Airavatesvara Temple**, which was built by the Cholas in the 12th century and has beautiful carvings, and the town of Swamimalai, a bronze-casting centre.

Kumbakonam can be visited en route from Chidambaram to Thanjavur. Temple 4km (2½ miles) west of town. Open: daily 6.30am–8.30pm. Free admission.

Thanjavur

The **Brihadishwara Temple** of Thanjavur is one of Tamil Nadu's architectural gems. The high *gopurams* are intricately carved but are dwarfed here by the pyramidal dome over the main shrine which soars about 65m

(213ft) over the plinth and is crowned by a carved cupola. Besides the profusion of imposing sculpture along the exteriors, the paintings inside are also noteworthy. The courtyard is lined with passages, including one which has 108 *lingams*.

The **Palace of the Nayakas of Thanjavur** now houses a museum containing a gallery of Pallava-, Chola-, Pandya- and Nayaka-period stone sculpture, glass paintings, some princely relics including a throne canopy, and an outstanding collection of about 400 bronze sculptures including some of the best Chola bronzes.

Brihadishwara Temple. Open: daily 6am–1pm & 3–8pm. Free admission.

Palace of the Nayakas. Open: 9am–6pm. Admission charge.
Thanjavur is connected by train to Chennai. It has hotels and restaurants.

Tiruchirappalli

Also known as Trichy, this busy town is dominated by its rock fort. Its main attraction is the **Ranganathaswamy Temple** at nearby Srirangam, which has exceptionally finely carved *gopis* and pillars dominated by equestrian sculpture.

Ranganathaswamy Temple. Open: daily 6am–1pm & 3–9pm. Free admission (camera charge).
Tiruchirappalli is connected by train to Chennai. It has hotels and restaurants.

Brihadishwara Temple is said to have been built in the 11th century by a Chola king

MADURAI
Madurai town

Madurai's Meenakshi Temple is not only considered to be one of the greatest sights of Southern India, but also one of the most impressive temples in the world. The town was a capital of the Pandyan dynasty until the 10th century, and it grew to become a centre of commercial trade, through the Tamil seaports, with countries as far-flung as China and Italy. Madurai is also known as a seat of Tamil culture, especially Sangam literature. The present temple building is credited to the Nayakas who took Madurai after it fell first to Islamic powers and subsequently to the Vijayanagara empire.

116km (72 miles) south of Tiruchirappalli, Madurai is served by flights and trains from Chennai.

Gandhi Memorial

This memorial museum is housed in a 17th-century palace of the Madurai Nayaka queens, which was converted by the British into an administrative building. The memorial exhibits Mahatma Gandhi's belongings, his bed, a model of his house at Wardha, paintings and photographs showing scenes from his life, and other relics. It also charts the history of colonised India and has a good account of the freedom struggle. In addition, the palace houses a government museum exhibiting bronzes, stone sculpture, Tanjore paintings, and folk art.

Tamukkam Palace. Tel: 0452 253 1060. www.gandhimmm.org; info@gandhimmm.org. Open: Thur–Tue 9am–1pm & 2–6.30pm. Free admission (camera charge).

Meenakshi Temple

The highlight of any visit to Madurai is the Sri Meenakshi Sundareshwara Temple, which is one of India's largest temples, both in terms of compound area and in number of shrines in a single enclosure. The four towering *gopurams* at the cardinal points are more than 43m (141ft) high, rising over huge entrances and carved with fine sculptures of deities, human figures and animals. Highlights of the temple include the Ashta Shakti Mandapam, with its sculpted columns depicting various aspects of Shiva and Shakti, and the tank surrounded by Nayaka murals illustrating the miracles of Shiva at Madurai. An 18th-century mural depicts the marriage of Meenakshi to Sundareshwara, while the Ayirakkal Mandapam (literally 1,000-columned hall) has more than 900 exquisite sculpted pillars as well as an art museum containing bronzes, sculptures and various temple artefacts. The Pudu Mandapam outside the east gate also has marvellously carved columns.

The temple is also an important pilgrimage site for Hindus, and, although the main shrine of Meenakshi is closed to non-Hindus, travellers can watch some rituals here.

Open: daily 6am–12.30pm & 4–9pm.
Free admission (camera charge).

Thirumalai Nayak Palace
This impressive palace was built during the reign of a famous Nayaka ruler, and at one time it had galleries, two royal apartments, theatre, temples, armoury and gardens. Much of its original structure was used by his descendants to build new palaces, but the hall of audiences, with its huge columns and a large dome, gives a good impression of how magnificent the original palace must have been in the 17th century.
Open: daily 9am–1pm & 2–5pm.
Admission charge.

SOUTHERN TAMIL NADU
Chettinad
This region, named after its Chettiar merchant community, has some of the grandest examples of domestic architecture in Tamil Nadu. The mansions of these merchants comprise successive blocks around courtyards, with carved wooden and granite columns, Italian marble floors, and velvety walls with egg-and-lime finish rising to gilded ceilings.
Some mansions at Karaikudi and Kanadukathan are open to visitors. These villages are on the route from Madurai to Thanjavur.

Kanyakumari
Named after a temple on the seashore, Kanyakumari stands at the meeting place of the Arabian Sea, the Bay of Bengal and the Indian Ocean. It is famous for its spectacular sunsets.
Trains from Thiruvananthapuram.

Rameshvaram
This sacred island in the Bay of Bengal is connected to the mainland by a bridge, the longest in Southern India. It is one of the holiest sites of pilgrimage for Hindus, revered as a *dham* or gateway of the Lord, and is associated with the *Ramayana*.
Trains from Chennai stop at Rameshvaram.

Ornate carving at the Thirumalai Nayak Palace

Andhra Pradesh

Lower-key than the other areas covered in this book, Andhra Pradesh, or AP to the cognoscenti, is an expansive state, the country's fourth largest by area and fifth largest by population. The 'rice bowl of India' has a rich history, both culturally and financially. Away from its Islam-influenced capital Hyderabad, an IT and movie hub, the state also has a sizeable tribal contingent, one of the many striking contrasts that are there for anyone who takes the trouble to look.

From 200 BC to AD 200 the Satavahana dynasty ruled over the area, and subsequently the medieval Kakatiyas reigned over the Telugu-speaking areas. The Nizams of Hyderabad, who were the richest rulers of India with the largest princely state at the time of independence in 1947, endowed the state with some of Southern India's most spectacular sites. These include the Buddhist community at Nagarjunakonda, as well as the impressive palaces, Islamic monuments and museums of Hyderabad. Andhra is also home to a great many magnificent forts, including Golconda Fort outside Hyderabad.

The Andhra capital of Hyderabad is still one of India's most important cities, largely by virtue of its recent growth as a hi-tech centre. Its emerging economy has encouraged investment by international banks and multinational corporations, as well as the IT centres of Cyberabad and Hi-Tech City. Already one of the six largest cities of India, the twin city of Hyderabad – Secundrabad – has an increasing buzz and modern feel around its plush residential localities and commercial centres.

The heart of Telugu culture can be found around the Godavari and Krishna delta regions, which are among the major rice-producing centres of India. These regions are known for their monuments, poets, artists and musicians. The riverbanks are at their greenest along the coast, where the estuaries' mangrove forests are particularly rich in birdlife and marine wildlife.

Also along the coast is the thriving city of Vishakhapatnam, a shipbuilding centre and port with a strong industrial base, but with beaches and hills nearby that provide welcome relief from the bustle of the city.

All this is in stark contrast to the arid and semi-arid Deccan Plateau of northern Andhra, known for its agricultural problems. It is best, therefore, to focus on the route east from Hyderabad to Vishakhapatnam across the Krishna and Godavari rivers.

A view of Hyderabad across the Musi River

HYDERABAD
Hyderabad city

One of India's largest cities, Hyderabad is a charming destination with lakes in and around the city, palaces, mosques and other buildings of interest erected during the reign of the Nizams. It also has bustling bazaars and one of Southern India's greatest forts at nearby Golconda. In contrast to the historic buildings of the city is the recently developed Cyberabad, with its Hi-Tech City, which has become the Indian base for many software development companies.

Hyderabad was laid out in 1591 by Sultan Mohamad Quli Shah on a grid pattern near his fortified citadel of Golconda. It became one of India's richest cities, and the grandeur of Hyderabad attracted Aurangzeb to besiege Golconda and take over the city for the Mughal Empire. As the Mughal power declined, the governor, Asaf Jah, began to exercise his independence; in 1724 he started a dynasty known by the honorific title of Nizam. The Nizam became the wealthiest rulers of India, but in 1948 their princely state was merged into India following military action. The last Nizam, Mir Osman Ali, was allowed to keep his treasures and was given a privy purse as compensation.

Nehru Zoological Park

This zoo, one of the largest in the country, is home to some 3,500 animals. Regular lion, tiger, bear and butterfly safaris are a highlight.

Nehru Zoological Park Road, to the south of the city. Tel: 0402 447 7355. www.hyderabadzoo.org. Open: daily Apr–June 8am–5.30pm, July–Mar 8.30am–5pm. Admission charge.

Ramoji Film City

An hour's bus ride to the southeast of the city, this large studio offers a delightfully kitsch tour plus lunch at a five-star hotel.
Tel: 0841 532 5856. www.ramojifilmcity.com. Open: 9.30am–5.30pm. Tours from 10am–4.30pm.

The Salar Jung Museum

The Salar Jungs were hereditary prime ministers in the Hyderabad court from the middle of the 19th century, and their collection, spanning three generations, was arranged by the third Salar Jung, Mir Yousuf Khan, who died in 1949. Great collectors of art and decorative objects, the Salar Jungs procured paintings, carpets, weapons, textiles, glassware, lacquer-work, bronzes, manuscripts and metalware from across India and also much further afield during their trips and through dealers. Some of their personal belongings, including clothes, utensils, books, furniture and photographs, are also exhibited in the museum. Textiles include hand-woven fabrics and *kalamkaris* (narrative paintings on cloth) of the kind still produced in Andhra. The museum also has a gallery devoted to Indian silk, cotton and woollen textiles, rich silver and gold hread brocades, and floral embroidery rom Punjab which is called *phulkaris*. The impressive ivory collection ncludes chess sets, figures, furniture nd other objects, all of them finely arved and some painted. The nuseum's collection of famous Bidriware', or ornate metalwork, of the Deccan, which still thrives in Hyderabad, includes hookahs, trays nd plates, and there is also a display of swords, daggers and gunpowder boxes with engraving, inlay work and other decorations on the handles or blades. The museum contains some interesting oil paintings by European and Indian artists, as well as miniature paintings representing various phases in Indian art from Jain palm-leaf paintings to Mughal miniatures and the Deccan School.

Salar Jung Marg, on the southern bank of the Musi River. Tel: 0402 452 3211. www.salarjungmuseum.in. Open: Sat–Thur 10am–5pm. Admission charge.

he ruined fort at Golconda

Walk: Markets and monuments around Charminar

The old city of Hyderabad was established on the southern bank of the Musi River in a grid pattern, with arched gateways and stone buildings housing shops and living quarters. The most attractive buildings are to be found south of the river. This area is best toured early before the markets get congested.

Allow 3 hours including sightseeing time.

Start at the southern end of the bridge across the Musi River.

1 High Court

Turn right from the bridge to see the High Court rising from the old gardens on the road running along the southern embankment of the Musi.

This was one of the architect Vincent Esch's best works in Hyderabad, with its Mughal façade built from pink granite with carved sandstone panels and columns, and surmounted by domes. Next to it the college, by Esch,

Bazaars surround Charminar

incorporates Gothic features and typically Indian pierced screens.
Walk back to the bridge and then take Sardar Patel Road south past the Charkaman, literally 'four arches', to the Charminar, passing a large market on the way.

2 Charminar

Literally 'four minarets', this yellow stucco building has been a showpiece of Hyderabad since it was built by Sultan Mohamad Quli Shah between 1591 and 1612. The four graceful minarets rise 56m (184ft) high, with spiral staircases leading to the upper storeys.
Open: daily 9am–5.30pm.
Admission charge.
200m (220yd) south of Charminar, turn right for the Mecca Masjid.

3 Mecca Masjid

This mosque was built in the 17th century by the Sultans and was completed by the Mughal emperor Aurangzeb. One of the largest in

Southern India, the red bricks over the arch are said to be made from Mecca clay. Next to the courtyard are the tombs of the Nizams.
Open: daily 9am–5pm (women not allowed).
Follow the road round from Mecca Masjid as it curves around Lad Bazaar, the market for bangles, pearl necklaces and Hyderabad's handicrafts. Southeast of Lad Bazaar, a lane leads to Chowmahalla Palace.

4 Chowmahalla Palace

Clustered around a quadrangle with a fountain as the centrepiece, the highlight is the elaborately decorated hall of audiences which houses the seat of the Nizam. The palace displays an extensive collection of textiles.
Tel: 040 2452 2032.
www.chowmahalla.com. Open: Sat–Thur 10am–5pm.
Retrace your steps to Charminar, and walk back to the bridge.

Hyderabad environs

Hyderabad makes a good base from which to visit two of Southern India's greatest forts, Golconda and Warangal. While Golconda is a short drive from Hyderabad, Warangal is a 150km (93-mile) drive or train journey and requires an early start for those who want to return to the city on the same day.

Golconda

The enormous fort of Golconda was founded in the 12th century as the mud fort of the Kakatiyas of Andhra and became the seat of power of the Sultans, who reinforced it with stone walls. After the court moved to Hyderabad, the fort was neglected until it was once again restored by the Nizams in the 18th century. The fort is famous for its three circles of fortifications at different levels, with the main double wall having 87 bastions guarded by cannons and pierced by eight gateways, four of which are in use, housing guardrooms between the outer and inner doorways. Successfully trading in diamonds, pearls and textiles, Golconda grew in importance and the vaults once housed some of the most famous diamonds in the world including, apparently, the Kohinoor. The carved teakwood Fateh Darwaja, the main entrance portico, has superb acoustics that enabled voices, claps, drum beats and bugle calls to be heard all around the fort.

From here the path leads to the beautiful arch of the mortuary bath where dead nobles were bathed before burial, the three-storey armoury and the *zanana* or palace quarters for the harem, where some floral carvings are still visible. Steps lead to the Durbarhall of the Sultans, with its rooftop pavilion overlooking the campus.

The fort was designed to withstand a siege; it has storehouses, water storage and an elaborate hydraulics system of clay pipes and Persian wheels to take water up to the palaces.
About 8km (5 miles) west of Hyderabad. Tel: 040 2351 3984. Open: daily 9am–6pm. Admission charge.
Sound and light show every evening; timings vary seasonally.

Qutb Shahi Tombs

The 54m (177ft)-high mausoleum of Sultan Mohamad Quli Shah is the most remarkable of about 82 tombs set in and around a garden near Golconda. Collectively the tombs form an attractive site, with their onion-shaped domes, plaster decorations on their granite or green stone walls, and delicate arches.
A visit can be combined with a tour of Golconda. Open: daily 9am–5pm. Admission charge.

Warangal

The citadel of Warangal was probably laid out during the reign of the Kakatiya rulers of the 12th and 13th centuries. The fort's remains consist of circular fortifications, with a moat round the older outer walls and ornate *rana* gateways that are still imposing. n the centre are the remains of a 12th-entury Shiva temple, and an audience all. The Kakatiyas were great patrons f architecture, and a mature example f the Chalukyan style of temple uilding can be seen at the temple on Ianamakonda hill, which has Shiva in the sanctum and shrines to Vishnu and the Sun God Surya, as well as beautiful carvings on the doorways, walls and pillars, rock-cut elephants and a large sculpted Nandi.

Open: sunrise–sunset. Admission charge. Warangal can be reached by train from Hyderabad. There are places to stay and eat in the town.

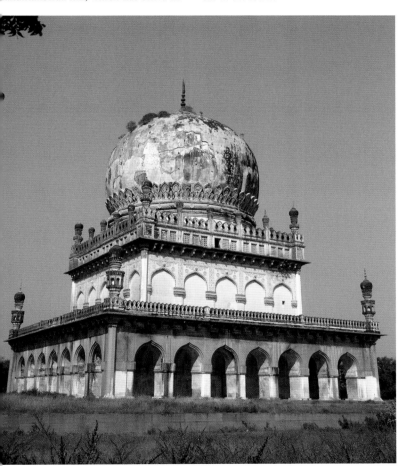

Mausoleum of Sultan Quli Shah at the Qutb Shahi Tombs

NAGARJUNAKONDA

Perhaps Southern India's richest Buddhist site, Nagarjunakonda was a highly cultured civilisation that stretched along the banks of the Krishna River during the reign of the Satavanas and became an important centre of artistic activity under the Ishvaku rulers of the 3rd century AD. It was a planned city, with rampart walls circling it on the three sides that were not protected by the river, and with wide roads, sanitary drainage, public baths and a number of residential areas.

After the Ishvakus were ousted by the Pallavas from Tamil Nadu, the site went into decline, but the opposite bank became the centre of Shiva worship during the reign of the Chalukyas from the 7th to the 12th centuries. The site also saw the development of a fort during the 15th and 16th centuries, when its control was contested between different kingdoms. A Vishnu Temple, five Shaivite temples, and Brahmanical shrines were among the remains found on this side of the Krishna River.

The site was discovered in 1926 in the Nallamalai or black hills beside the River Krishna; prehistoric and protohistoric remains, Buddhist monuments and other relics had remained undisturbed for some 1,600 years. The original site is now buried under the reservoir created by the Nagarjuna Sagar Dam, but the important remains were relocated and reconstructed on a hilltop that is now an island on the artificial lake.

Nagarjuna Sagar is about four hours' driv southeast of Hyderabad. There are places to stay and eat along the embankment. Launches leave for the island from Vijayapuri, on the banks of the Nagarjun Sagar daily at 9.30am & 1.30pm.

Anupu

Near the eastern embankments of the Dam, Anupu is the site of the reconstruction of an amphitheatre, which could seat about 1,000 people and had superb acoustics, suggesting a interest in music and performing arts. Some people also believe that this site has connections with Rome. Here you will also find *stupas*, and a *vihara* that is believed to have been a Buddhist university during the 2nd century AD.

Nagarjunakonda Museum

The highlight of the museum on the island site is the 3m (10ft) standing Buddha. Also found here are friezes showing episodes from the life of Buddha, including his mother's vision of an elephant and a lotus blossom, his renunciation of worldly affairs, and his enlightenment. The Buddha statues show various postures, including teaching and meditation. Columns are richly carved with Buddhist scenes, elephants and lotus motifs, and there are also memorial columns with secula themes dedicated to rulers, artisans and religious leaders. The museum also exhibits Neolithic tools, metal axes and knives, beads, coins, caskets, ritual

nding Buddha at Nagarjunakonda Museum

nsils and ornaments found at the
. More recent exhibits from the site
lude 13th-century Jain sculptures
17th- to 18th-century statues of
esha, Nandi, Shiva and Shakti. The
seum also has a model of the
inal site.

*n: Sat–Thur 9.30am–3.45pm.
rges for admission and
aunch.*

Stupas

The earliest structure on the island was
probably the Maha-chaitya uncased
stupa, renovated in the 3rd century AD
by the Ishvaku princess Chamtisiri
and believed to house relics of the
Buddha. Nearby, a towering Buddha
statue stands over the remains of a
monastery foundation, which also has
a small *stupa*.

VIJAYAWADA

Two of the three great rivers of Southern India, the Krishna and the Godavari, flow through Andhra Pradesh to create a delta region called both 'the rice bowl of Southern India' and 'the granary of Andhra'. The towns here have made the area the most important for Andhra culture, producing some of the most famous Telugu authors.

Amravati

Once an important centre for Buddhism, Amravati saw the art of the Krishna delta reach its zenith in the 2nd century AD. This was the site for ancient Chintapalli, where a *stupa* was erected on the relics of the Buddha during the reign of the Mauryan emperor Ashoka. Ashoka converted to Buddhism in the 3rd century BC after seeing the death and destruction of Kalinga in his own quest for conquest, and Chintapalli was enlarged during the reign of the Savahanas from the 1st century AD onwards. The *stupa* has gone, but its base gives an idea of its size and circumference, and some scenes from the life of Buddha can still be seen. The ground plans of the monastic quarters remain at the site.

Most of the relics have been moved to the **Government Museum of Chennai** (*see pp102–3*) as well as to the Indian Museum of Kolkata and the British Museum in London; however, a handful remain at the site's archaeological museum (*open: Sat–Thur 10am–5pm. Small admission charge*). Here exhibits show various stages of development of the site from the 3rd century BC to the 12th century AD, and they include panels, railings and a number of sculptures. The sculptures comprise one of Buddha in his teaching posture with lotus symbol on his feet, curled hair and long earlobes; Tara, a Bodhisattva; and depictions of the *bodhi* tree – some of which are really fine – as well as chakras and lotus symbols. The collection also has relic caskets, pottery, coins and bangles from Amravati, and finds from other excavations in the Krishna district. A model of the *stupa* shows how it must have looked 2,000 years ago.

Rajahmundry

Rajahmundry, on the Godavari River, is known for its poets. Nannayya, often called the first poet of Telugu literary history, is credited with starting the translation of the *Mahabharata* into Telugu, building the vernacular vocabulary required for the Andhra *Mahabharata* about 1,000 years ago. It is also the home of author Kandukuri Veeresalingam, who brought about a revolution in the social structure of Andhra in the 1800s and 1900s. He campaigned for the rights of widows to remarry, and he opposed child marriage and the dowry system. He is credited with writing the first Telugu drama, and he also wrote the Telugu novel, *Rajasekhara Charitra*, as well as prose specifically for women.

Damerla Rama Rao Art Gallery at the Parade Grounds, though now looking rather uncared for, displays works by the late Andhra Pradeshi artist Damerla Rama Rao who died in 1925, and the gallery also hosts temporary art exhibitions. The **Government Archaeological Museum**, also known as the Rallabandi Subbarao Museum, *(Godawari Bund Rd. Open: Sat–Thur 10.30am–5pm. Free admission)* has an interesting collection of sculpture, about 450 manuscripts (some of which are made of palm leaf), copper plates, Satavahan pottery, various coins, and archaeological finds from excavations in the Godavari district.

Rajahmundry has an airport and a railway station. There are places to stay and eat in the town.

Vijayawada

The headquarters of the Krishna district, Vijayawada is named after the **Kanaka Durga Temple** (*Indrikila Hill. Open: daily 5am–9pm. Free admission*) whose presiding deity is also called Vijaya. The **Victoria Jubilee Museum** (*Bandar Rd. Tel: 0866 257 4299. Open: Sat–Thur 10.30am–5pm. Nominal admission charge*) has finds from sites of the Krishna delta, while the nearby **Ondavalli Caves** (*open: 9am–5pm. Admission charge*) exhibit 6th- and 7th-century columns and sculptures in niches.

240km (149 miles) southeast of Hyderabad, Vijayawada has an airport and a railway station. There are hotels and restaurants in the town.

Inside the Ondavalli Caves

Getting away from it all

The Southern States afford plenty of opportunities to escape from India's often overwhelming urban hustle and bustle. If you find solace in a soothing Ayurvedic massage, Kerala is the epicentre of the discipline, although treatment centres also abound elsewhere. Those seeking to commune with nature have a plethora of serene lakes, remote hill stations, and enviable birdwatching sites to explore, while the many wildlife reserves allow visitors to witness the animal kingdom at close quarters.

KERALA

It is easy to escape the crowded towns and tourist centres of Kerala by taking an Ayurvedic programme, a houseboat cruise or a tour of wildlife reserves.

Ayurvedic resorts

A number of resort companies and hoteliers have developed health resorts to make the most of the popularity of Ayurvedic massages (*see pp34–5*).

Houseboats

Few visitors return from Kerala without taking a boat trip on the backwaters (*see pp40–41*). One means of travelling the backwaters is by chartered houseboat, which allows more flexibility to plan an itinerary than tour boats and ferries.

The price is based on the route, the facilities and services, the duration of the cruise, the size of the houseboat, the number of rooms, and the meals. Trips usually start at Alappuzha, Kollam, Kottayam or Kumarakom, but other stretches, such as the backwaters near

Thiruvananthapuram, Kozhikode and Bekal, are also good for cruising. *Government tourist offices and tour operators can be contacted to book a houseboat. Hotels and resorts of Kollam, Alappuzha and Kottayam district usually have their own houseboats or can arrange one according to your requirements.*

Sanctuaries and National Parks of Kerala

Aralam Wildlife Sanctuary

This sanctuary, now being developed, is home to elephants, mouse deer and sambar deer, besides a range of birds. *Near Kannur. Contact the Aralam Wildlife Division, Irrity, Kannur District. Tel: 0490 249 3160. www.aralam.org; wildlifewarden@aralam.com. Open: daily 8am–4pm.*

Chinnar Wildlife Sanctuary

The Chinnar sanctuary comprises mainly deciduous forests and scrub flora. Permission to stay at the forest rest houses is hard to obtain, and most

visitors make the trip from Munnar or stay in simple highway hotels near Marayoor.
See p67 for more information.

Eravikulam National Park
The highlight of the 97sq km (37sq mile) Eravikulam National Park is the Nilgiri tahr.
See p66 for more information.

Idukki Wildlife Sanctuary
This sanctuary is home to elephants, gaur bison and dhole wild dogs. You can stay at Kottayam, 20km (12½ miles) away.
Tel: 0486 223 2271.

Kumarakom Bird Sanctuary
Set along the Vembanad Lake, this bird sanctuary is home to darters, cormorants, herons and egrets, and attracts migratory birds in winter.
Tel: 0481 252 5864. Open: daily 6am–5.30pm. Admission charge. See p43 for travel details.
Resorts at Kumarakom arrange boating and houseboats to tour the sanctuary.

Neyyar Wildlife Sanctuary
The 128sq-km (49sq-mile) Neyyar sanctuary has a reservoir offering boat safaris. The sanctuary has elephants, tigers, bears and Nilgiri langurs, but permission must be sought for trekking. Basic meals and accommodation are available locally.
Tel: 0471 227 2182.
Regular buses to Neyyar from the KSRTC bus stand in Thiruvananthapuram.

Kerala Tourism Development Corporation runs a hotel and cafeteria near the dam. Boats can be hired for a tour of the lake.

Parambikulam Wildlife Sanctuary
This 285sq km (110sq mile) sanctuary is one of the finest places to view gaur (Indian bison) in Southern India. Accommodation is available, while some visitors make a trip from Coimbatore or Palakkad, both more than 100km (63 miles) away.
Open: daily 7am–6pm (last entry 4pm). www.parambikulam.org; wildlifewarden@parambikulam.org. Admission charge. Bus: daily or twice daily from Pollachi, Parambikulam and Topslip.

Peechi-Vazhani Wildlife Sanctuary
This sanctuary's 125sq km (48sq miles) of forest is a good place to watch 60 species of birds including waterfowl. The mammals include elephants, tigers, panthers and deer. The floral diversity includes 50 species of orchid.
Buses run to Peechi Dam from Thrissur. Permits from the Wildlife Warden at Thrissur.
Tel: 0487 228 2017.

Peppara Wildlife Sanctuary
This 53sq km (20sq mile) sanctuary, near Thiruvananthapuram, has a fine reputation as a spot for birdwatching.
About 50km (31 miles) from Thiruvananthapuram. Contact the District Forest Office.
Tel: 0471 232 5385.

Getting away from it all

Periyar National Park
Periyar is one of the leading tiger reserves of India. It is set around a reservoir.
See p60.

Shenduruny Wildlife Sanctuary
The Shenduruny moist deciduous forests, 66km (41 miles) from Kollam, span an area of about 100sq km (39sq miles). On the banks of the Shenduruny River are Mesolithic painted caves.
Contact The Wildlife Warden, Shenduruny Wildlife Sanctuary, Thenmala Dam PO, Thiruvananthapuram. Tel: 0475 234 4600.

Silent Valley National Park
This prime rainforest of 90sq km (35sq miles) is well known for its endangered monkeys and is best visited between December and April. Palakkad, 85km (53 miles) away, has accommodation.
Tel: 0492 422 2056. Open: daily 8am–5pm (last entry 2pm). Admission charge.

Thattekkad Bird Sanctuary
One of the best bird sanctuaries in Kerala, on the banks of the Periyar River in Ernakulam district.
Tel: 0485 258 8302.
Open: Oct–Apr 6am–6pm.
Admission charge.

Wayanad Wildlife Sanctuary
An impressive sanctuary of forests, swamps and grasslands.
See p81.

KARNATAKA
With its beaches, spas and wildlife reserves, all easily accessible from the popular tourist destinations of Bangalore, Mysore, Madikeri and Hampi, Karnataka makes a great destination as an escape from the more frenzied sightseeing itinerary.

Ayurveda, spas and health centres
Bangalore is the hub of India's health tourism industry, with spa resorts in and around the city offering Ayurvedic and other Indian treatments. Some also offer Thai, Balinese, Chinese and European treatments. Ayurveda and natural treatments are growing in popularity, and resorts and hotels at other destinations, such as Mysore, Mangalore, Kodagu and Hampi, have developed their own massage and treatment centres for travellers.

For more serious yoga and naturopathy programmes, the **JSS Institute of Naturopathy and Yogic Sciences** (*www.jssinys.org*) at Jindalnagar outside Bangalore, is highly regarded.

Some interesting websites:
www.angsana.com (Angsana Oasis Spa Resort, Bangalore)
www.goldenpalmshotel.com (spa resort near Bangalore)
www.soukya.com (centre offering Ayurveda, homeopathy, naturopathy, yoga, reflexology, acupressure, acupuncture and other treatments at Whitefield, Bangalore)

www.ayurvedagram.com (Ayurvedic resort at Whitefield, Bangalore)
www.theleela.com (luxury hotel chain with spas and Ayurvedic centres)
www.summer-sands.com (beach resort with massage facilities at Mangalore)
www.ayurindus.com (Ayurvedic centre at Mysore)

Beaches

The stretch of coast between the Western Ghats and the Arabian Sea is followed by the Konkan Railway line and National Highway 17, which both travel the entire length of the Karnataka coast. This area is also known as the Sapphire Coast of India, and the route offers access to some of Southern India's prettiest beaches.

Devbagh Island

This island, 3km (2 miles) offshore from **Karwar** at the confluence of the Kali River and the Arabian Sea, is a must for beach lovers. It has log hut accommodation.
Karwar is on the main Konkan Railway line.

Gokarna

Gokarna's famous **Om Beach** is named after its curving stretch of sand in the shape of the Hindu *Om*, while **Kudle**, **Half Moon** and **Paradise beaches** are also popular. Gokarna is also a popular place of pilgrimage for Hindus.
Gokarna has a railway station, hotels and restaurants.

Mangalore

Sandwiched between one of the wettest stretches of the Western Ghats and the coastline, Mangalore is known for its busy port, industry, terracotta tile factories and colleges. It is also an interesting place to view historic monuments, including 10th-century temples, a 15th-century church, and a

The beach at Murdeshwar near Gokarna

chapel with frescoes, as well as museums housing archaeological finds. Mangalore has a handful of popular beaches, such as nearby **Ullal**.
Mangalore has an airport and a railway station. There are good hotels in town and a resort at Ullal beach.

Udupi

Udupi is one of the most important Vaishnavite centres on the southwest coast of India. It is the birthplace of Madhva, a saint who set up monasteries in the town in the 13th and 14th centuries. The centre of religious activity here is the Krishna Temple.

A short drive from Udupi is the fishing port of **Malpe**, which is associated with Vasco da Gama. The explorer is said to have landed at St Mary's Isle and set up a cross before his historic landing at Kappad in Kerala.
Udupi is on the main Konkan Railway line.

Waterfalls

Jog Falls is Southern India's highest waterfall. Altogether, it consists of four falls, the longest dropping about 253m (830ft), although the dam on the Sharavati River has reduced the flow. The falls are set in the spectacular countryside of the Western Ghats, being particularly impressive shortly after the monsoon, and the jungle-carpeted hills are a great place to do some hiking.
Jog Falls is about 2^{1}/$_{2}$ hours' drive from Hanovar Railway Station.

Wildlife reserves

Karnataka has five national parks and over 20 wildlife sanctuaries, including some of the most spectacular in Southern India. The hills are an important habitat for elephant, tiger and other endangered wildlife, and the following sanctuaries have been developed for tourism.

Bandipur National Park

This large national park is part of the **Nilgiri Biosphere Reserve**, along with **Madhumalai** (also spelt Mudhumalai) in Tamil Nadu (*see pp139–40*), **Wayanad** in Kerala (*see p81*) and Nagarhole (*see p136*), comprising an important wildlife corridor, especially for herds of elephants.
Tel: 0822 923 6021. Open: daily 6–9am & 4–6pm. Admission charge.
Bandipur is about 90km (56 miles) from Mysore. There is a good choice of accommodation, ranging from basic forest rest houses to privately owned wildlife resorts.

Bannerghata National Park

A popular day excursion from Bangalore, part of this national park has been developed for recreation, with a zoo, drive-through safari-park enclosures with big cats and herbivores, and picnic facilities. The surrounding forests are inhabited by a variety of mammals and birds.
Tel: 0802 842 9366. Open: 9am–5.30pm. Admission charge.
Bannerghata is about 26km (16 miles) south of Bangalore.

Bhadra Wildlife Sanctuary

This wildlife sanctuary, situated in the wet forests along the Bhadra River, has been declared a Tiger Reserve, but it is notoriously difficult to spot one of these wonderful, elusive animals. Otters and crocodiles are often seen at the Bhadra Reservoir, while drives through the sanctuary could well result in sightings of elephants, gaur (Indian bison), a variety of deer and monkeys, and many species of birds. Leopard sightings are also possible.

Tel: 0826 223 4904; dcfbhadra@ yahoo. com. Open: daily 6.30–9.30am & 3–6pm.

Bhadra is 153km (95 miles) north of Mangalore. There is accommodation near the reservoir.

Biligiri Rangaswami Hills

The **Biligiri Rangaswami Temple Wildlife Sanctuary** mainly comprises deciduous forests with patches of scrub and grassland, becoming increasingly evergreen at higher altitudes. While driving through the sanctuary, visitors stand a good chance of seeing elephants, sambars, spotted deer, wild boar and gaur, and occasionally also leopards and sloth bears. The sanctuary is also an excellent place for birdwatching, and you can expect to see eagles, thrushes, flycatchers and numerous other species.

Tel: 0822 622 2059. Open: 6am–6pm. The temple sanctuary is about 86km (53 miles) from Mysore, with accommodation at K-Gudi nearby.

Dandeli Wildlife Sanctuary

This 475sq km (183sq mile) sanctuary is one of Southern India's most popular rafting destinations, with white-water and scenic raft trips organised on the Kali River. The river flows through moist deciduous and semi-evergreen forests, and ibises, darters and storks are likely to be sighted while on the river. Other bird species, such as hornbills, sunbirds, parakeets, woodpeckers and barbets, can often be spotted while walking or driving in the forests. Elephants, gaur, bonnet macaques, langur monkeys, giant squirrels and leopards (including black mutant) could well be sighted here, and there is also a resident population of tigers.

Open: daily 6am–6pm. www.dandeli.com. Dandeli is 125km (78 miles) from Londa on the Konkan Railway line. There are resorts and campsites near the Kali River.

Daroji Bear Sanctuary

This small sanctuary makes a good day excursion from Hampi, having a substantial sloth bear population in its scrub-forested hills. Bears are often

Sambar deer can be seen in many of Karnataka's reserves

sighted from the watchtower, below which there is a waterhole, and there are also chances of seeing wild boar, monitor lizards, jackals, Indian foxes and a number of species of scrubland birds. The sanctuary has been declared an Important Bird Area by the Indian Bird Conservation Network because of the presence of the yellow-throated bulbul, which is a globally threatened species.

Open: daily 6am–6pm.
Admission charge.
Daroji is about 20km (12 miles) from Hospet, which has places to stay and eat.

Rajiv Gandhi National Park, Nagarhole

Like Bandipur, this national park is located at the meeting place of the forested hills of Kerala, Karnataka and Tamil Nadu. Elephants, sambar deer, spotted deer, wild boar, gaur and hares are often seen during drives through the park, and there are also chances of seeing sloth bears, leopards and even tigers. As far as birdlife is concerned, Malabar pied hornbill, green imperial pigeons, grey jungle fowls, red spurfowls, crested serpent eagles, parakeets and flycatchers are regularly seen in the area. Large herds of elephants can usually be spotted at the Kabini River, especially in summer, and crocodiles, freshwater turtles, darters, cormorants and herons are other possible sightings from the coracle boats that are available for hire.

Rajiv Gandhi National Park.
Tel: 0821 248 0901. Open: daily 6–9am & 3–6.30pm. Admission charge.

Nagarhole is about 94km (58 miles) from Mysore. There are wildlife resorts and lodges at various places in the park, including Karapur near the Kabini River.

Ranganathittu Bird Sanctuary
See p91.

TAMIL NADU

Rising from the coast to the peaks of the Western Ghats more than 2,500m (8,200ft) above sea level, Tamil Nadu offers a number of scenic resorts which provide relief from the bustle of its large industrialised cities and its crowded temple towns.

Andaman and Nicobar

Just over 1,000km (621 miles) offshore from the Tamil coast, the islands of Andaman and Nicobar have some of India's finest beaches and coral reefs, and they are popular diving and snorkelling destinations. Most of the islands are thickly forested with tropical vegetation.

The arrival point by air and sea is **Port Blair**. The town has a jail with 698 cells where freedom fighters from India were imprisoned. It now houses a museum containing various instruments of torture, and it has nightly sound and light shows on its history. Port Blair also has an aquarium, an anthropological museum, a forest museum and a maritime museum, all of which are good primers for visits to the other islands. There is a popular beach at **Corbyn's Cove** out of town, and the road from here continues to **Chiriya**

Tapu, with its pleasant beach and forested trails. Operators offer trips in glass-bottomed boats, as well as diving and snorkelling encounters in the bays and islands, including protected marine reserves, with boat transfers out of Port Blair. Another popular excursion is to **Mount Harrier**, reached by ferry from Port Blair. Here a forested path leads past tall tropical trees hung with vines, and it is an excellent spot for birdwatching and butterfly spotting, while the view from the summit is breathtaking.

The most popular island for relaxing is **Havelock**. Here **Radhanagar Beach** is regarded by many as India's finest. Reached by a road through forests, the beach has perfect white sand with calm waters rich in marine life.

Port Blair jail. Open: Tue–Sun 9am–12.30pm & 1.30–5pm. Nominal admission charge. Planes operate between Chennai and Port Blair, which has a good choice of hotels. From here, passenger ferries connect to Havelock Island, which has a few good places to stay.

Hill resorts

The **Nilgiris** or Blue Hills of Tamil Nadu are home to some of Southern India's most famous hill resorts. Developed for tourism, **Ooty** and **Kodaikanal** both provide a pleasant break from the plains, while those looking for peace and quiet can head for the tea-plantation town of **Conoor** or the coffee-plantation town of **Yercaud**.

Kodaikanal

At an altitude of about 2,100m (6,890ft) above sea level, Kodaikanal offers superb views of the hills. The centrepiece of Kodaikanal is its star-shaped lake, which is extremely popular for strolls, cycling and boating. Next to the lake, **Bryant Park** has paths meandering among attractive assortments of flowers and trees. The **Croaker's Walk** offers breathtaking views of the Nilgiri Hills, and the granite cliffs called **Pillar Rocks** are another natural attraction.

Getting away from it all

The countryside around Ooty

Popular excursions from Kodaikanal include **Fairy Falls** and **Bear Shola Falls**, and there is also a natural history museum on the road to **Madurai** that is worth a brief stop.

At one time a hill retreat for American missionaries and the British officers working in Tamil Nadu, Kodaikanal has attractive colonial-period houses. It is now a very popular hill resort for the people of Tamil Nadu and Kerala, and it can get very crowded during holidays.

Kodaikanal is about 120km (75 miles) northwest of Madurai's airport. The city has a good choice of places to stay and eat.

Udagamandalam (Ooty)

Ooty is one of the best-known hill resorts in Southern India. At an altitude of about 2,200m (7,218ft), it was the summer retreat for most British residents of Southern India. While the town is now built up and can get rather crowded with visitors during holiday periods, there are still some quiet corners where peaceful walks are possible.

The **Botanical Gardens** are one of the town's main attractions. Laid out in the 1840s by gardeners from London, they sprawl over 16ha (40 acres) with a wide variety of trees and flowering plants that are a blaze of colour. The large lake attracts visitors who enjoy the area's walks and boating opportunities. The colonial buildings include **St Stephen's Church** and **Civil Court**, while the **Ooty Club** has been a centre of sports and recreation since the 1840s – the rules of snooker are said to have been laid down here.

The main natural attractions are outside Ooty town. **Dodabetta** is the highest peak of Tamil Nadu and can be seen from the road to **Kotagiri** from Ooty town. At just over 2,600m (8,530ft) above sea level, the summit has a viewing tower that provides a breathtaking view.

Southeast of the peak is **Conoor**, a town surrounded by tea-planted slopes. Less congested than Ooty, it is a delightful place to take a stroll, and it retains a strong hint of the British Raj with its colonial bungalows and plantation houses. Botanists should head for **Sim's Park**, which has an excellent display of flowers, as well as an attractive lake that you can walk around. There are good views from **Dolphin's Nose** near **Catherine Falls**, as well as from **Lamb's Rock**, and it is possible to get permission to visit some of the tea estates around town.

Another tea planters' town is **Kotagiri**, nearly 2,000m (6,561ft) above sea level, with good views of the surrounding hills. It is particularly known for its handicrafts.

Botanical Gardens. Open: daily 8am–6.30pm. Admission charge.
St Stephen's Church. Open: Mon–Sat 10am–1pm & 3–5pm. Services Sun 8am & 11am. Free admission.
Sim's Park. Open: daily 8am–6.30pm. Admission charge.

Ooty is easily accessible by road from Coimbatore airport. The city has a good choice of places to stay and eat.

Yercaud

The town of Yercaud, in the **Shevator Hills**, is surrounded by coffee estates and fruit orchards. It is a good place for walking and trekking, with some very fine strolls around the lake.

Yercaud is easily accessible by road from Salem railway station.

Wildlife reserves

Tamil Nadu has a particularly rich diversity of wildlife habitats, ranging from the **Marine National Park** in the Gulf of Mannar, and the bird-rich saltwater lagoons along the coast, to the forests of the Nilgiris that are home to a fantastic variety of animals, birds and plant life.

Indira Gandhi National Park (Anamalai Hills), Topslip

Some of Tamil Nadu's finest forests are in this wildlife reserve. Some 958sq km (370sq miles) in size, the park's vegetation ranges from dry deciduous to evergreen and even shola (or swamp) rainforest. It forms an almost uninterrupted forest area with **Parambikulam** to its west and the **Eravikulam National Park** and **Chinnar Wildlife Sanctuary** to its south, all three in Kerala. This large forest corridor has created a habitat for endangered wildlife such as the Nilgiri tahr and the lion-tailed macaque, one of Southern India's

rarest monkeys. Most visitors to **Topslip** stand a good chance of spotting elephants, gaur (Indian bison), a variety of deer, the Nilgiri langurs and bonnet macaques, and there are also resident tiger and leopard populations that are, understandably, a little more difficult to find. The park is good for birdwatching, with resident species including the Sri Lankan frogmouth, white-bellied treepie, Malabar trogon, white-bellied blue flycatcher and numerous others.

Tel: 04259 222 5356. Open: daily 6.30am–6pm. Admission charge.

Topslip is about 75km (47 miles) from Coimbatore airport.

Madhumalai National Park & Wildlife Sanctuary

Tamil Nadu's most popular wildlife reserve, Madhumalai forms part of an important wildlife corridor with **Bandipur** and **Nagarhole** in Karnataka, and with **Wayanad** in Kerala, forming what is called the **Nilgiri Biosphere Reserve**. Mainly deciduous forest in the rain shadow of the Western Ghats, the sanctuary was for some time disturbed by an elusive poacher called Veerappan, but has since recovered. Large herds of

Herons are common around Vedanthangal Bird Sanctuary

elephants can sometimes be seen, including some old individuals with really long tusks, while gaur are Madhumalai's pride as they are known to reach an exceptional size here. Spotted deer are easily seen in good-sized herds, and wild boar are abundant. The sanctuary also harbours tigers, leopards, wild dogs, flying squirrels, Malabar flying squirrels and other wildlife, but sightings of these are not easy. Together, Madhumalai and Ooty form a very interesting area for birdwatchers, especially for those who want to see the flycatchers of the Nilgiris.
Tel: 0423 252 6235. Madhumalai is accessible from Coimbatore, and it has a good choice of accommodation.

Pulicat Bird Sanctuary

This large saltwater lagoon is renowned for its abundant flocks of flamingos, ducks, storks, avocets, sandpipers and other birds.
About 90km (56 miles) north of Chennai.

Vedanthangal Bird Sanctuary

This small reservoir is one of Southern India's most spectacular birdwatching sites. A path through the wetland area offers views of large flocks of spoonbills, open-billed storks, grey herons, night herons, pelicans, darters, cormorants and numerous other birds that nest in the acacia trees. In the winter months the tank makes a very good spot to observe migrating ducks.
Tel: 0442 432 1471. Open: 6am–6pm. Nominal admission charge.

Vedanthangal is 86km (53 miles) south of Chennai. It is also a popular excursion from Mahabalipuram or Kanchipuram.

ANDHRA PRADESH

With a wide diversity of landscapes, from the Eastern Ghats to its long coastline, Andhra presents a number of attractive getaways from the densely populated regions of Hyderabad, Vishakhapatnam and the river deltas.

Beaches

The most popular beaches are those near **Vishakhapatnam**. It is a good idea to ask locally before entering the sea, as many stretches of the Bay of Bengal are not safe for swimming.
Vishakhapatnam has an airport and a railway station. There is a good choice of hotels in the city, as well as places to stay at Rishikonda, a popular beach. The museums and old buildings in the city, and the Buddhist sites nearby, are also worth a visit.

Birdwatching

Andhra's wetlands and grasslands are excellent birding areas. Below are some of the best sites near tourist destinations.

Hyderabad's lakes

Hussain Sagar is a large lake with a colossal granite Buddha, one of the world's largest freestanding Buddha statues. **Shamirpet**, about 28km (17 miles) away, is a good place to watch storks, spot-billed ducks and

Cattle grazing at Shamirpet Lake

other water birds. Other lakes, among them **Osman Sagar**, are popular recreational spots around Hyderabad.

Kolleru Lake
This large lake, with its neighbouring marshes, attracts a diversity of waterfowl.
Kolleru can be visited as a day excursion from Vijayawada.

Pakhal Lake
This large lake, situated in a deciduous forested sanctuary, supports large flocks of waterfowl.
Pakhal Lake is about 60km (37 miles) east of Warangal.

Pulicat Lake
This large lagoon is one of the top winter habitats on the east coast of India for shore birds, and it is a good place to see species such as spot-billed pelicans, greater flamingos and painted storks.
The lake is near the Chennai–Nellore Highway and can be visited as a day trip from either.

Rollapadu Wildlife Sanctuary
An important habitat for blackbuck or Indian antelope, many species of grassland birds can be seen here, as well as raptors such as eagles and the great Indian bustard.
Rollapadu is near Kurnool, which has places to stay and eat.

Hills
Araku
Araku offers access to a number of coffee estates and tribal villages in the Eastern Ghats, and it is also home to one of Andhra's best tribal museums. Also visit the **Borra Caves**, with their spectacular stalactites and stalagmites, en route to Vishakhapatnam.
Tribal Museum. Open: 10am–1pm, 2–5pm. Nominal admission charge. Borra Caves. Open: 10am–5.30pm. Admission charge. Araku is a scenic drive or railway journey (on one of the world's highest broad-gauge lines) from Vishakhapatnam. There are places to stay at Araku and Tyda on the road to Vishakhapatnam.

Horsley Hills
Situated at about 1,200m (3,937ft) above sea level, among the deciduous forests of the Eastern Ghats, this resort is a popular destination for walks, weekend trips and birdwatching.
About 140km (87 miles) from Tirupati, a temple town with an airport (soon to be international) and railway station. Horsley Hills has places to stay and eat.

Shopping

Shopping in India can be an exciting experience. The four states featured in this book have a rich tradition of handloom weaving, metalwork, wood and stone carving, and other handicrafts, as well as arts such as painting and contemporary sculpture. Southern India also grows high-quality spices, tea and coffee.

How to shop

At established shops, prices are generally fixed and there is no real room for bargaining, although some shops will give you a deal for large purchases. It may be a good idea to check the prices at different shops before buying, as the discounts may vary. Shops usually announce 'clearance sales', 'discount sales', 'off-season sales' and 'festival discounts' in the newspapers or declare them on banners.

At street-side markets and at flea markets the prices are usually marked up and there is considerable room for bargaining. In tourist centres, vendors generally hike the price up and you might do well by halving the asking price and then reaching an agreement. Walk away slowly in order to gauge the response of the vendor, and you will usually be called back for further negotiation. Shop owners and sales people can be very persuasive, so it is important to be firm and not be swayed.

What to buy

Southern India is known for its textiles, such as the silk sarees of Mysore in Karnataka, the silk sarees and brocades of Kanchipuram in Tamil Nadu, the ikat-woven cotton and silk sarees of Andhra Pradesh, and the silk and cotton fabrics from the northern districts of Kerala.

The tradition of metal sculpture continues at bronze-casting workshops in central Tamil Nadu. Bidriware, the art of engraving on a metal alloy before blackening and polishing, was developed in Bidar in Karnataka by Persian artisans from the Sultan's court. Attractive boxes, vases and other items are produced at Hyderabad in Andhra Pradesh.

Mahabalipuram is India's stone-carving capital, and high-quality sculptures, mainly Hindu idols, are produced in its workshops. Wooden items range from the painted toys of Kondappali and Ettikopakka of Andhra and Chennapatnam near Bangalore, to the fine ebony, rosewood and sandalwood sculptures of Karnataka.

Jewellery is another popular buy, especially in the markets of Hyderabad, where pearl necklaces and locally made glass bangles are sold, and in Tamil Nadu, known for its silver ornaments. For jewellery made from precious metals and gemstones, it is best to buy from larger shops that will certify that they are genuine.

Andhra Pradesh is also known for folk narrative paintings on both cloth (Kalamkari) and on furniture (Nirmal). Tribal artefacts made from bamboo and terracotta can be bought at Araku in Andhra, and the embroidery of the Lambani Banjara community can be purchased in Hampi, in the northern districts of Karnataka, and in parts of Andhra. For contemporary art, the galleries in the major cities have exhibitions, and auctions from time to time.

Southern India is also a good place to buy spices such as cardamom, cinnamon, ginger, pepper and nutmeg, and tea and coffee. These are available at shops, markets and estate outlets. Vendors in Kerala also sell attractive packs of spices that make good souvenirs or gifts.

Pondicherry is known for its fine handmade paper, and for a range of other crafts.

It is illegal to take genuine antiques out of India without proper licensing, but you can find good copies in the markets.

Where to buy

Government-owned emporia are generally safe bets for genuine quality at fixed prices, but sometimes private shops also claim to be government emporia. Hotel shopping malls and big shops also guarantee quality, although they may be more expensive. Some non-governmental organisations (NGOs), registered charities, communes and artisans' cooperatives have retail outlets promoting the work of artisans or disadvantaged people.

Some factories are open for visitors to see their processes, such as weaving, coir-making or tea production; it is then possible to buy from the factory outlet.

There is no dearth of markets in India. They are good places to look for fresh fruits, vegetables, meats and fish, and to find bargains.

Old city bazaars are atmospheric and full of colour, and the maze of streets and alleys is lined with vendors, open-air stalls and shops selling a wide range of products for the locals, including utensils, jewellery, clothes and food.

KERALA
Kochi
Art
Chitram Art Gallery
MG Road, Ernakulam. Tel: 0484 235 7012.
Dravidia Art & Performance Gallery
Bazaar Road, south of customs jetty. Tel: 0484 309 6812.
Galleria Synagogue
Mattancherry. Tel: 0484 222 2544.

Kashi Art Gallery
Burgher Street, Fort Cochin. Tel: 0484 221 5769. www.kashiartgallery.com

Books
DC Books
Kurian Towers, Banerji Road, Ernakulam. Tel: 0484 239 1295. www.dcbooks.com
Idiom Books
183 Synagogue Lane, Jew Town. Tel: 0484 222 5604.
Paico *MG Road, Ernakulam Business Centre. Tel: 0484 235 5835. www.paicoindia.com*

Handicrafts
Kairali
MG Road. Tel: 0484 235 4507.

Jewellery
Alapatt Fashion Jewellery
MG Road, Ernakulam. Tel: 0484 235 2149.
Temple Fashion Jewellery
2330 Muthodt Royal Square.

Textiles
Parthas Textiles
PB 1774 MG Road. Tel: 0484 237 4175.

Thiruvananthapuram
Books
DC Books
Statue Junction. Tel: 0471 245 0133.
Higginbothams
Building No. 25/2339-42, MG Road. Tel: 0471 233 1622.

India Book House
MG Road. Tel: 0471 247 5443.
Modern Book Centre
Near GPO, MG Road.
Prabhat Book House
Vanchiyoor. Tel: 0471 247 1533.

Handicrafts
Gift Corner
Pazhavagadi.
Handloom House
Powerhouse Road. Tel: 0471 247 2886.
Kairalai
Opposite Secretariat. Tel: 0471 247 5627.
Natesan's Antiqarts
Opp. Ayurveda College, MG Road. Tel: 0471 233 1594.
Partha's
Powerhouse Road. Tel: 0471 246 1949. www.parthastvm.com; info@parthastvm.com
SMSM Institute
YMCA Road. Tel: 0471 233 0298.

KARNATAKA
Bangalore
Books
Gangarams
72 MG Road. Tel: 0802 558 1618.
Higginbothams
74 MG Road. Tel: 0802 558 6574.
LB Publishers
90–91 MG Road.
Motilal Banarasidass
236 III Block, 9th Main Road, Sri Ranga, Jayanagar. Tel: 0802 654 2591. www.mlbd.com
Prism Books
11th Main Road, IV Block, Jayanagar.

Tel: 0802 663 7527.
www.prismbooks.com

Handicrafts
Cauvery
49 MG Road. Tel: 0802 558 1118.
www.cauverycrafts.com
Central Cottage Industries Emporium
144 MG Road. Tel: 0802 558 9515.
www.cottageemporium.in

Textiles
Deepam Silk
67 MG Road. Tel: 0802 558 8760.
**Karnataka Silk Industries
Corporation**
Jubilee Showroom, 44/45 Leo Complex,
Residency Road Cross.
Tel: 0802 558 2118. www.ksicsilk.com;
info@ksicsilk.com
Mysore Saree Udyog
294, 1st floor, K Kamraj Road.
Tel: 0802 558 3255.
www.mysoresareeudyog.com;
info@mysoresareeudyog.com

TAMIL NADU
Chennai
Books
Higginbothams
814 Anna Salai. Tel: 0442 851 3519.

Handicrafts
Gujurat Emporium
New No. 13 (old No. 67) Royapettah
High Road. Tel: 0442 498 4440.
SIPA's Craftlink
Kodambakkam High Road,
Nungambakkam. www.sipa.in

Spencer Plaza
G47, ground floor, Anna Salai.
Tel: 0442 849 1001.

ANDHRA PRADESH
Hyderabad
Books
AA Hussain & Co
5-8-551 Abids Road, Abids.
Tel: 0402 320 3724.
Bookionics
3-5-1114/7, opp. Hotel Traveller,
Kochiguda. Tel: 0402 475 3654.
Higginbothams
Near Lal Bahadur Stadium,
Fateh Maldan.
Walden
Greenlands Road, Begumpet.
Tel: 0402 340 3344.

Handicrafts
Lepakshi
Opposite telephone exchange,
Musheerabad. Tel: 0402 766 8178.
www.lepakshihandicrafts.gov.in

Textiles
Pochampally Silks and Sarees
Tilak Road. Tel: 0406 673 5216.
www.pochampally.com

Ayurvedic powders used in Hindu rituals

Arts and crafts of Kerala

Patronised by the princely states and temple builders, the artists and artisans of Kerala excelled in painting and sculpture.

Painting

The painting traditions that began in rock-cut temple caves more than 1,000 years ago reached their zenith in the temples of the 16th to the 18th centuries, such as Ettumanoor, the palace of the Rajas of Kochi, and even in the churches of Kerala. Drawing heavily from the style of the Pallava, Hoysala and Vijayanagar School, these murals were distinctive in their use of colour, line and subject matter.

Some people believe that the origins of Keralan mural painting can be traced back to *Kalamezhuttu*, ritual drawings of deities and *mandalas* (geometric patterns), made with coloured powder. Each colour derives from natural sources such as rice flour, turmeric, leaves and burnt husk, and is applied using the thumb and forefinger.

Sculpture

Like painting, woodcarving developed in Kerala with patronage from the landed families and the temple builders. Sandalwood, teakwood and rosewood sculpture, especially those of Hindu deities, can be seen in a number of cities and towns. Toys, lacquered woodwork, Kathakali models and wooden furnishings are sold at emporia and in the markets.

Metalwork

The traditional medium for metal sculpture is a blend of gold, silver, copper, iron and tin (called *panchaloha*), but bronze sculptures of deities also became popular because of their durability. Bell metal, comprising mainly copper, is commonly used today for metal crafts, such as temple bells, which are said to have a special chime when struck. One of the most famous centres for metalwork is

Carved sandalwood figures

Shiva images are available all over Southern India

Nadavaramba, near Irinjalakuda, which manufactures oil lamps and cooking utensils.

Gold jewellery

For the people of Kerala, gold symbolises light, eternity, wealth and purity. Gold jewellery is therefore present at auspicious occasions, particularly births and weddings. In the past, the design of the jewellery often denoted the community to which the wearer belonged, but now patterns are universal and range from the plain to the elaborate. The Nagapadam is a serpent pendant, once popular with Nair women, and generally in the shape of a cobra hood. The Kasumala is a gold coin necklace, usually depicting the Goddess Lakshmi, although some Kasumalas also portray British royalty.

The Tali necklace tied around the neck of a bride has an Om if she is a Hindu and a cross if she is Christian. The Cheruthali necklace is an ornament of the Namboodiri Brahmin women, and the Oddiyanam waist belt is extremely popular among Tamil Brahmins. The Vanki is a forearm ornament generally used during weddings, while gold earrings, especially the bell-like jhimka, are also popular in Kerala. The Mekka Mothiram was a popular ornament of the Christian community in Kerala, and the Mangamala is a necklace with a mango motif. The jasmine-shaped pendant is called a Mullamottu, and the Palaka is a gold ornament set with green glass. The jewellers of Kerala rarely set other stones into gold jewellery, and although contemporary designs are coming into fashion, most of them are still based on traditional patterns. No visitor to Kerala, especially to the central region from Kochi to Kozhikode, can fail to notice the number of hoardings advertising gold jewellery.

Other handicrafts

Kerala is well known for weaving of various kinds, including coir weaving, reed weaving, screw-pine mat weaving, and grass mat weaving, as well as embroidery and lace making. Some weaving units have started using jute as a substitute to coir and cane.

Entertainment

*Entertainment in Southern India generally revolve
around traditional performances of dance drama,
Carnatic music and Kerala's martial arts, Kallaripayettu.
In the modern cities of Bangalore, Hyderabad and
Chennai, rock and jazz bands, Latin American dances and
other international performance arts are becoming
popular at luxury hotels, nightclubs, lounge bars and pubs.*

ART GALLERIES

The art galleries in the museum complex
at Thiruvananthapuram hold regular
exhibitions of contemporary artists.
Kochi has exhibitions and performances
at the **Galleria Synagogue**, the **Dravidia
Art & Performance Gallery** and **Kashi**.

CINEMA

India has one of the world's largest film
industries. While Hindi films transcend
regional borders, doing well in most
states of India, regional language films in
Andhra Pradesh, Tamil Nadu, Karnataka
and Kerala are also extremely popular.
Film stars have achieved almost cult
status in the south; some have even been
elevated to the levels of gods. The films'
popularity has made the actors politically
influential and some have won positions
in government assemblies. They are often
called upon for canvassing during state
and national elections.

An Indian film is usually a larger-
than-life escapist fantasy, though in
recent times stories have become more
realistic. While tragedies were popular
in the early years of the Hindi film
industry, the 1970s and 1980s saw the
advent of 'masala movies', which
followed set formulae that appealed
across cultural boundaries. Common
themes were: a hero, the 'angry young
man', fighting evil against all odds with
a love interest thrown in; a reunion
between brothers separated during
childhood; or one of the 'love triangle'
themes involving two friends in love
with the same girl, with one making the
'supreme sacrifice' for his friend.

Spanning three hours including an
interval, a typical Hindi film features a
little of everything – romance, comedy,
action, melodrama, religious piety and
song sequences at the drop of a hat,
usually filmed in spectacular settings
such as snowy peaks, desert dunes or
beaches. Many films are shot in
foreign locations.

Today, the film industry is going
through something of a revolution with
film makers targeting the Hindi-

peaking audience in the UK and USA,
nd in other countries where tickets are
nore expensive than in India and
DVDs are in greater demand. The
ncreased revenues have resulted in
etter production standards and more
ubtle storylines.

As Hindi films continue to be
popular, there is usually a cinema hall
 or near every city or town. The
andards of cinema halls are improving
 the larger cities like Chennai,
yderabad and Bangalore, with many
w multiplexes offering more legroom
d more comfortable seats.

Thiruvananthapuram hosts an
nual International Film Festival
ww.iffk.keralafilm.com), and the city
s many cinemas showing Indian films,
well as some English-language films.

CULTURAL CENTRES FOR MUSIC, DANCE AND FOLK ARTS
Kochi
Cochin Cultural Centre

*Sangamam, Manikath Road,
Fort Cochin. Tel: 0484 235 6366.
www.cochinculturalcentre.com. Email:
director@cochinculturalcentre.com.
Daily performances at 6.30pm.*

Greenix Village

*Kalvathy Road, Fort Kochi.
Tel: 0484 221 7000. www.greenix.in.
Email: info@greenix.in. Daily
performances at 6.30pm.*

Kerala Kathakali Centre

*Opposite Brunton Boatyard, KB Jacob
Road, Fort Cochin. Tel: 0484 221 5827.
www.kathakalicentre.com.
Email: vijayan@kathakalicentre.com.
Daily performances at 6pm.*

Entertainment

n poster in Kollam

See India Foundation

Kalthil Parambil Lane, Ernakulam.
Tel: 0484 237 6471.
Daily performances at 6pm.

Bangalore
Nrityagram Dance Village
Hessaraghatta. Tel: 080 2846 6313.
www.nrityagram.org.
Open: Tue–Sat 10am–2pm.

Chennai
Kalakshetra Arts Village
Thiruvanmiyur. Tel: 044 2452 4057.
www.kalakshetra.in.
Open: 8.30–11.30am.
Music Academy
New No. 168 (Old No. 306), TTK Road.
Tel: 044 2811 2231.
www.musicacademymadras.in

Hyderabad
Shilparamam Arts Crafts and Cultural Society
Madhapur, Hi-Tech City. Tel: 040 6451
8164. www.shilparamam.org. Open:
daily 10.30am–8.30pm.

Kalaripayattu
It is possible to see students learning the martial art of Kalaripayattu or masters practising at gymnasiums called *kalaris* in almost every town in Kerala. Demonstrations are often available if advance notice is given (the price is based on the number of people attending). You can also book Ayurvedic treatments. Short courses are run at some *kalaris.*

CVN Kalari
Nadakkavu, Kozhikode. Tel: 0495 276
9114. www.cvnkalarikerala.com.
Email: sunilkalari@yahoo.com
CVN Kalari Sangham
East Fort, Near Sri Padmanabhaswamy
Temple, Thiruvananthapuram.
Tel: 0471 247 4128.
ENS Kalari
Embram Madam, Nettoor, Ernakulam,
Kochi. Tel: 0484 270 0810.
www.enskalari.org.in

Kathakali
One of the four main classical styles of India, the dance drama follows certain norms but is dynamic and has accepted various changes over the years, such as replacing the mask with stiff make-up. In order to make the dance drama form more popular, shorter versions have been created for tourists.

The ritualised dance drama form of Kathakali is performed at the temple theatres of Kerala, but these are rarely open for non-Hindus. A good alternative, however, is to see a performance at a cultural centre.

Hotels at Thiruvananthapuram, Kovalam and Kochi also stage Kathakali shows on a regular basis: ask at the tourist offices for information.

Music
Kerala is known for its Carnatic music, and you should be able to find out about performances in all the major cities. Ghazals and other Hindustani music is popular in Kozhikode.

NIGHTLIFE

Conservative Southern India is not famed for its wild nightlife; partygoers generally head for Goa. There are a few postprandial options, though, notably in the big cities and Kerala's tourist resorts. Kovalam and Varkala are the liveliest resorts, despite the alcohol restrictions to which most establishments there are (at least theoretically) subject.

Bangalore

Despite the official closing time of 11.30pm imposed by local law, Bangalore is something of a nightlife hub. Some establishments impose a cover charge that can usually be redeemed against purchases inside.

Beach
Coastal-themed bar and restaurant.
211, 100 Feet Road, HAL 2nd Stage, Indranagar. Tel: 080 4126 1114. www.kpgroups.in

NASA
Take a space odyssey into this quirkily decorated, popular bar.
1/4 Church Street. Tel: 080 2558 6512. Open: 11am–11pm.

Taika
Upmarket eatery by day, two attached but different clubs by night.
The Pavilion, 62–63 MG Road, Church Street. Tel: 080 4151 2828. Open: 8am–11pm.

Chennai

Chennai has a few nightlife options – in hotels and subject to a midnight curfew.

10 Downing Street
British-theme bar with pub-type wood, leather upholstery and 'Maggie' and 'Major' signs above the ladies and gents.
North Boag Road, Thyagaraya Nagar. Tel: 044 2815 2152. Open: 6–11pm.

Leather Bar
Dark, intimate bar at one of the city's most stylish hotels.
The Park Hotel, 601 Anna Salai. Tel: 044 4214 4100. Open: 6–11pm.

Hyderabad

The nascent nocturnal scene in the Andhra Pradesh capital also ends at midnight. Cover charges may apply and solo males are sometimes barred.

Liquids Again
Swanky nightspot frequented by the Hyderabad great and good.
5th Floor, Bhaskar Plaza, Road No. 1, Banjara Hills. Tel: 040 6625 9907. Open: 11am–11pm.

Kochi

The Armoury
It's more about the home-made cakes and tea by day, but the range of alcoholic tipples and harbour-side spot make this atmospheric after dark.
Brunton Boatyard, Fort Cochin. Tel: 0484 221 5461. Open: 7.30am–10.30pm.

Loungevity
A rare chance to strut your stuff in Kerala's first designer bar. Eclectic music and funky décor.
39/2026 The Avenue Regent, MG Road, Ernakulam. Tel: 0484 237 7977. Open: 7pm–late.

Children

India is a family-oriented society where children are welcomed, and this warmth is extended to those travelling with them. Children are very popular in India and most Indians will bend over backwards to help you. They are welcomed in most hotels and restaurants, religious places and at the various tourist sites and monuments. However, travelling with children in India does involve a few hazards of which you need to be aware.

Accommodation

It makes sense to find a good hotel for your base while in India. Most chefs will prepare food to your requirements and there is usually a minibar with bottled water and snacks. Hotels will happily supply an extra bed or a family room at a supplement, although children below the age of ten are not usually charged for occupying a room. Some hotels and resorts are geared up for children, with play areas, toddlers' pools, indoor games, movies, competitions and special menus, but it is best to find out about the facilities when you book. Some hotels may be able to arrange babysitters.

Food

It may be a good idea to carry baby food with you, particularly if your child has particular favourites which may not be available. At hotels, resorts and restaurants there is generally a large menu, with good options for children.

Eggs, biscuits, bread, butter, cheese, chocolate, bottled drinks, ice cream, packaged and canned foods are generally available everywhere.

Health

Those travelling with babies and children need to be careful. Besides all the necessary vaccinations (*see pp183–4*), children should also be protected against diphtheria, whooping cough, mumps, measles and Hepatitis B.

Local people love children and will offer them sweets and fruits, so it is important to be vigilant about this when travelling with children. It may help to explain to them that the child has to be on a special diet when travelling in India.

On the road

Long journeys with children in India can be difficult – not least because of the hazardous driving practices and parlous state of some roads, which can rn even a relatively short journey into protracted nightmare – so it's best to ase yourself in just one or two places. you are renting a car, buying a child's ir seat is a good idea. Bathrooms are irely clean; taking a portable toilet seat ith you may help. There are grocery ores by the roadside, and snacks are vailable on board the trains, but it's est to pack some snacks for your urney. Biscuits, chocolates and soft rinks are easily available.

acking

appies and toiletries are available Indian cities, but emergency ipplies are recommended. Also, ake sure you bring any medicines hich you may need, as well as a rst-aid kit. It is a good idea to ack some toys and books to keep ildren amused.

Things to do

India does not have any of the large amusement parks that children look forward to visiting. However, children will probably enjoy the general liveliness of India, where getting around in auto-rickshaws, trains, ferries and chartered boats can be fun. Rides on elephants, camels, ponies and boats are also great favourites.

Backwaters

Cruising the backwaters can be great fun for children, and speedboats can also be hired for short journeys.

Beaches

Children will enjoy the beaches of Kerala and Karnataka. Kovalam is a popular beach destination, while beaches at Veli and Varkala near Thiruvananthapuram, Marari near

ochi schoolgirls playing near Santa Cruz Basilica

Alappuzha, and those near Kochi, Thallesseri, Kannur and Bekal in Kerala, and near Mangalore and Gokarna in Karnataka are also popular for day trips. Before entering the water, check that it is safe to swim or paddle there; some beaches have lifeguards who will show you the safest areas.

The beaches along the Bay of Bengal coast of Tamil Nadu and Andhra Pradesh are generally less safe for swimming than those on the west coast of India, but they are very pretty (*see pp133–4*).

Hill resorts

Children are likely to enjoy hill stations such as Ooty and Kodaikanal that have lakes with boating facilities, pony riding trails, bicycle hire, parks and gardens. Hotels at these hill resorts are usually geared up for children, as they are very popular with Indian families.

In town

All cities and towns have parks and gardens, with paths for a pleasant stroll and with areas for children to play.

Shopping

The Indian bazaars and handicraft emporia can be fun for children. Locally made dolls dressed in the attires of different states of India, Kerala's papier mâché Kathakali masks, handcrafted wooden toys and miniature boats are favourites. However, make sure that the toys you buy are safe for children.

Wildlife reserves

Seeing big animals is exciting for children. The launch tours at Periyar Lake can be thrilling, especially in the morning or evening when elephant herds, gaur, sambars, bears, monkeys, fishing eagles and turtles are most likely to be seen. Drives in Wayanad in Kerala, Nagarhole, Bandipur and the Biligiri Rangaswami Hills in Karnataka, and Madhumalai in Tamil Nadu also offer good opportunities to see elephants, a variety of deer and monkeys, and possibly even a leopard or tiger. Coracle rides with the locals on the Kabini River in Karnataka are also enjoyable, as they can get closer to elephants and crocodiles. There are good accommodation options at the reserves. Check the safety regulations at each park, as it may not be safe to venture into certain areas.

Zoological parks

Hyderabad has one of the best zoos in Southern India, with large enclosures, drive-through safari parks to see big cats from mini-buses, a nocturnal house, a reptile park and a café. Mysore's zoological park also has well-designed enclosures that re-create the natural habitat of each animal or bird. Other important zoos are at Chennai, Thiruvananthapuram and Vishakhapatnam. Chennai also has a well-known snake park at Guindy, a wooded park in the city where deer and other animals can be seen, and a crocodile park.

street vendor selling whistles

Sport and leisure

Although sports are not generally associated with India, except, of course, for Himalayan mountaineering and cricket, they are nevertheless a popular form of entertainment. All kinds are on offer, from spectator sports to those especially developed for tourism, such as watersports and adventure activities.

Large hotels and resorts have sports facilities including swimming pools, and many smaller ones have indoor games facilities such as pool tables. The clubs are the best places for sports and leisure, but entry is usually restricted to members. Some clubs have reciprocal arrangements with those elsewhere, while some offer temporary membership, and hotels may be able to arrange admission to a club nearby. Some clubs also have residential rooms, which can be an alternative to staying at hotels, but you may need to be introduced by a member. You could also ask about government-run sports facilities that are open to the general public.

Sports facilities
Adventure and watersports
Dandeli National Park in Karnataka is a popular destination for rafting, canoeing and kayaking on the River Kali. The rafting activities on offer range from scenic floats through the forests, which are good for birdwatching and occasional wildlife sightings, to strenuous white-water rafting at the falls. There are resorts and camps near the entrance to the national park run by Indian Adventures (*www.indianadventures.com*) and Jungle Lodges and Resorts Ltd (*www.junglelodges.com*).

Angling
Some hotels and resorts have their own ponds, private lakes or backwater inlets where they allow fishing on catch-and-release or you-catch-we-cook basis. Most of them have fishing rods, but it may be a good idea to bring your own. The prized fish of the Kerala backwaters is *karimeen*.

The High Ranges Angling Association at Munnar is helpful in giving information and obtaining licences for fishing in Kerala's lakes and rivers. Most globetrotting anglers visit Southern India to fish for the mahseer, a group of carp that ranks among the

rgest and toughest freshwater fish in
ne world. Permits to catch the mahseer
re usually given on a catch-and-release
asis, as this is an endangered group of
sh. Jungle Lodges and Resorts Ltd
perates camps at mahseer fishing sites
n the Kaveri River. The resorts and
amps in Kodagu district can also help
nthusiasts to get permits from the
egion's wildlife association for
nahseer fishing.

asketball

asketball is a popular game, mainly at
chool and college level.

illiards and snooker

illiards and snooker are enjoyed in
ndia. Most clubs have a billiards room
nd some hotels have pool tables.

Cricket

Cricket is the most popular sport in
India. Crowds gather in hotels and
public places to watch international
fixtures on TV, especially if the Indian
team is playing. You can observe
cricket practice at stadiums and on
campuses, as well as informal games
played on open ground, and children
playing with a bat and ball even in
narrow streets. You may even be
invited by locals to join a friendly
game. At competitive level, cricket is
a serious business, and Indian clubs
invite foreign teams to play or tour
other countries. All the four states in
this book have cricket associations.
Some of India's leading test and one-
day international players are from
Bangalore and Hyderabad.

olleyball at the roadside in Thrissur

You can play cricket on any surface

Cycling

Southern India offers a variety of terrain for bicycle touring. Indian bicycles are good for short distances and local sightseeing, but they are not very comfortable for serious touring on hilly roads or rocky paths. You can either join a group tour with everything taken care of by the operator, or bring your own bicycle, preferably a mountain bike. If you bring a bicycle, carry more spares than you think will be needed, including oil and a pump.

Indian bicycles can be hired at most cities, towns and villages at very nominal prices. Imported bicycles are available only at very popular tourist destinations.

Football

Football is a popular sport in Kerala. Its football clubs excel in national tournaments, and they usually also have members in the national team.

With the advent of international TV channels in India, football is widely followed, and most locals will discuss the last World Cup if they know you have any interest in the game.

Golf

Kerala has some seven- to nine-hole golf courses and one or two 18-hole ones, but admission is usually reserved for club members and their guests. The Trivandrum Golf Club's clubhouse was established about a century ago by the

Maharaja of Travancore. Munnar has golf courses for the plantation staff and management, and local hotels may be able to help you find a local member who can introduce you as a guest. Bangalore and Kodagu district in Karnataka, and Ooty in Tamil Nadu, have golf courses but similar restrictions may apply. Bangalore has a number of 18-hole golf courses, including the historic Bangalore Golf Club founded in 1876, the Karnataka Golf Association's course and the Eagleton Resort. Hyderabad, Chennai and Mysore also have 18-hole golf courses and others have been mooted. You can find out about any local tournaments that allow foreigners to participate.

The Trivandrum Golf Club, Kowdiar, Thiruvananthapuram. Tel: 0471 243 5834. www.trivandrumgolfclub.com.
High Range Club, Munnar. Tel: 0486 523 0253. www.highrangeclubmunnar.com.
Cochin Golf Club, Bolgatty Island. Tel: 0484 275 0908. www.cochingolfclub.com

Scuba diving and snorkelling

Visitors to Southern India in search of good diving sites and unspoilt marine areas for snorkelling may find them in Lakshadweep, a cluster of islands offshore from Kerala, or at Andaman off the eastern coast of India. For those visiting Lakshadweep, there are flights from Kochi that land at Agatti, from where the resort on Bangaram Island generally arranges helicopter or ferry transfers for their guests.

Port Blair on South Andaman Island receives flights from Chennai. Most Port Blair hotels can arrange snorkelling trips and there are tours from the harbour to some of the good reefs nearby. Dive operators usually have offices or booking agents at Port Blair or at Havelock Island.

Check a company's certification and safety standards before joining a tour or course.
Bangaram Island Resort, Lakshadweep (CGH Earth, Kochi. Tel: 0484 301 1711. www.cghearth.com). The Society for Promotion of Nature Tourism and Sports in Lakshadweep, Willingdon Island, Kochi. www.lakshadweeptourism.com

Swimming pools

Almost all resorts and most of the big hotels have a swimming pool. By regulation, swimming pools at Indian hotels and resorts are shallow and prohibit diving. They have separate changing rooms, with showers, for men and women. Towels are provided and many hotels have smaller pools for children, as well as Jacuzzis® next to the main pool. Pools are cleaned regularly, and it is a good idea to follow the specified swimming pool opening times to avoid chemicals and soaps. Some hotel pools permit non-residents, for an admission charge.

Swimming pools at clubs and sports complexes usually follow

international competitive standards regarding size and depth, and many have diving boards.

Tennis, badminton and squash

Most of the bigger resorts and hotels and almost all clubs have facilities for these popular games. Tennis and badminton are very popular in Bangalore, Hyderabad and Chennai.

Volleyball

Volleyball is enjoyed in Tamil Nadu and Kerala, and is also played at school and college level in the other states of India. Some beaches also have volleyball courts for visitors.

Health clubs and spas
Ayurveda, yoga and meditation

With the increasing international interest in these ancient Asian disciplines for physical and spiritual wellbeing, several hotels and resorts have made yoga, meditation and Ayurvedic therapies available to their guests. Both short- and long-term courses are offered, and at some upmarket resorts there are daily sessions for beginners at fixed hours.

For more serious yoga students, the beginner and advanced courses at ashrams and government-approved institutions may be preferable. Neyyar near Thiruvananthapuram, and Nileshwar near Kasaragod, are among the most renowned places for yoga instruction.

See Neyyar under Thiruvananthapuram on p30.

Health clubs

Many hotels and resorts have health clubs with a gym, sauna and steam bath. Use of the gym is usually free for hotel residents. Most health clubs are managed by a team of supervisors responsible for maintaining the equipment and assisting guests. A few hotels and resorts also have daily aerobics sessions and weight-training instructors. The health clubs generally have separate sections for men and women, but some may also have different timings.

Long-staying visitors can also become members of health clubs with qualified instructors. Inspect the equipment and hygiene standards before joining a programme.

Birdwatching

Birdwatching in Southern India is particularly rewarding. The long coastline of Andhra Pradesh and Tamil Nadu is very good for spotting flamingos, pelicans and shore birds. The Coringa Wildlife Sanctuary comprises mangrove forests at the estuary of the Godavari, and you can also spend time at the large lagoon of Pulicat, the lagoons and salt pans of Point Calimere (Kodikkarai), 94km (58 miles) from Thanjavur, and the lagoons of Rameshwaram Island.

The Western Ghats offer excellent birding opportunities, especially at:

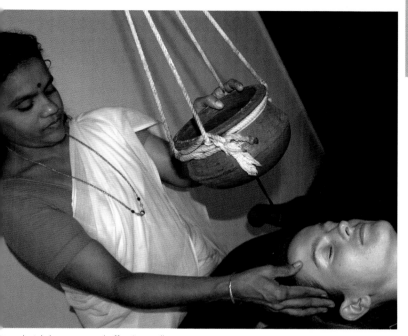

ome hotels have spas and offer Ayurvedic massage

he hill stations of Ooty and Kodaikanal, where many species haracteristic of the Nilgiri hills can e seen; Munnar and its nearby vildlife reserves; the Nilgiri Biosphere Reserve stretching from Madhumalai hrough Bandipur and Nagarhole to Wayanad; Periyar Lake and its urrounding wildlife reserve; and the alim Ali Bird Sanctuary off the Kochi–Munnar highway.

Ranganathittu Bird Sanctuary and Kokarebellur near Mysore, and the Vedanthangal and Karikili wetlands ear Chennai, are good places to get lose-up views of breeding birds. Kollapadu is perhaps the best

sanctuary in Southern India to see the Great Indian Bustard, and is also home to the endangered Lesser Florican. The sanctuary is one of the largest roosting sites for harriers in Southern India.

Walking
Southern India offers plenty of variety for those who love walking. There are narrow roads through the old quarters of most cities and towns, village paths that offer a glimpse of rural Indian life, coastal roads through palm groves, winding roads and paths in the hills, mountains and in plantation areas, and more strenuous treks in the Western Ghats.

Food and drink

Visitors will find a delightful variety of food in Southern India. While seafood such as crab, lobster, crayfish, prawns, shrimps, squid, clams and mussels are abundant on the Arabian Sea and Bay of Bengal coasts, you will also find lamb, mutton (goat), beef, pork, chicken and duck and a variety of fresh vegetables, cooked in the locally grown spices.

Where to eat

Indian food can be a lot more spicy on its home ground than at curry restaurants abroad; Indians use chillies liberally. Hotels, resorts and restaurants in the tourist centres are accustomed to travellers and usually prepare food to suit the foreign palate. The cooks are pretty accommodating about preparing food according to any specific dietary or special requests. Many hotels used by package operators serve buffet meals. This is not to everyone's taste, but can be a good way to sample new foods without risk.

Outside the big hotels and restaurants, it is generally safe to eat where the food is freshly prepared and well cooked, including the street-side *dhabas*.

Health issues

One of India's greatest health hazards for visitors is its drinking water. Drinking straight from a tap, or using tap water for cleaning teeth, is an open invitation to water-borne diseases, as the public water supply is often contaminated. Bottled water is widely available, but check the seal properly and crush the bottle before disposing of it so that it can't be refilled. At restaurants, ask for the sealed bottle to be opened in front of you. If you are visiting someone's home, ask if the water is 'purified'. Carry water sterilisation tablets and a filter if you are planning on going off the beaten track where bottled water might not be available.

Fruits, vegetables, cold meats and fish that have been exposed to flies or washed in dirty water are risky even in big hotels. Shellfish is not recommended unless you know that it is very fresh.

Drinks

Tea, or *chai*, is made in Indian homes and restaurants by brewing tea leaves, milk, water and sugar. This is usually a safe drink to have, and it is often easily available at street-side kiosks, railway stations and on trains. *Masala chai* includes powdered spices such as ginger, cardamom or cinnamon. Hotels and restaurants used to having a lot of foreign visitors are more likely to serve tea with milk and sugar separate.

In the same vein, coffee is also served white, brewed with milk and sugar unless specified in local outlets, but the more upmarket or tourist-oriented places will do it in the international style. Espresso and cappuccino are becoming popular at cafés and coffee shops, and Southern India is famous for its local-style filter coffee.

Another popular beverage in India is *lassi* or *chaas*, which is buttermilk made by churning yoghurt. As this contains water, exercise caution in cheaper establishments. Similarly, make sure that fruit juices are served without water or ice.

Alcohol does not have the same place in Indian culture as it does in the West. Kerala in particular has strict licensing laws, under which the cost of serving drink legally prices out most smaller establishments. Some, in tourist hotspots like Kovalam, have various cunning ways to circumvent the legislation, such as serving beer in mugs or from teapots or asking customers to keep bottles under their seats. Others simply don't serve alcohol. Those nonplussed with the idea of a 'dry' holiday can either use their duty free allowance when arriving or head for the more upmarket hotels, almost all of which are fully licensed and serve a range of local drinks and often international beverages – albeit often at international prices.

Many tourists enjoy trying out the local tipples. Much Indian beer – Kingfisher is the big name – is of good quality. Indian wine can be hit and miss, but decent bottles are available. Only the hardy of constitution should tackle the local spirits, such as Kerala's *feni*, a potent palm wine.

Breakfast

At hotels, breakfast is usually a lavish buffet, but it can also be a set American, Continental or Indian menu. Even at smaller hotels, packaged cereals with milk, fried eggs or omelettes and buttered toast form the usual breakfast spread, with a further choice of North Indian or South Indian breakfast items.

If you are eating out at street-side restaurants, the usual breakfast options are *puri* (deep-fried wholewheat rounds)

Limes for sale in Kollam

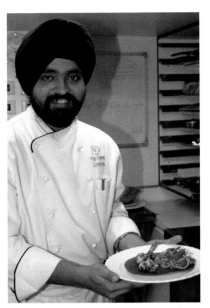

The chef on the *Oberoi Vrinda* motor vessel puts on a cookery demonstration (*see p174*)

with vegetables, *parathas* (Indian wholewheat bread cooked and usually stuffed with potatoes and other vegetables), *idlis* (rice dumplings), *wadas* (deep-fried savoury doughnuts) or *dosas* (savoury rice pancakes, usually stuffed with potatoes, and served with a lentil soup, *sambar*, and a coconut chutney).

Indian food

Tandoori is very popular in the Southern States; this refers to marinated mutton, chicken or fish barbecued in an earthenware oven and usually served as kebabs or *tikkas*. The main courses of a North Indian meal (also called Mughlai or Punjabi and usually listed separately on restaurant menus) are rich, with

liberal use of cream and nuts. The South Indian restaurants and cafés are usually owned by the Brahmin community and serve pure vegetarian food, which means they do not serve eggs or alcohol, although concessions are made in places likely to attract tourists. *Udupi*, generally associated with authentic Brahmin cuisine of the Karnataka coast, is commonly seen as a prefix or suffix to the name of eateries across the Southern Indian states. These are good places to get not only popular snacks but also a set meal of vegetables, *rasam* (peppery soup), *sambar* (lentil soup, usually with a coconut base), dumplings, pickles, chutneys, apalams or papadums, rice and sweets like *payasa* (rice pudding) or *holige* (fritters). Most *Udupi* food is made without onions or garlic.

Darshinis are Southern India's regional fast-food cafés serving inexpensive South Indian snacks and meals. They are very popular in Bangalore. Mangalorean restaurants are strong on seafood cooked with a coconut base. Kodagu district is known for its pandi curry (pork) and rice dumplings. 'Tiffin Rooms' at Bangalore, Mysore and other cities are known for their excellent *masala dosa* (potato-stuffed crisp pancakes) for breakfast and set meals.

Andhra's *bhawans* or restaurants offer a variety of food from across Andhra Pradesh, ranging from Hyderabadi food which is strongly influenced by the Middle-Eastern and Mughal origins of the Nizams of Hyderabad, to the food of the fertile Krishna and Godavari deltas, that of the drier areas of the Deccan, and the coastal cuisine around Vishakhapatnam. Typical meals or *thalis* at these *bhawans* are hot and spicy with lots of chillies and pungent pickles as accompaniments, though you could ask for milder versions in the tourist areas. The meals usually contain a lot of leafy vegetables. A sour-tasting leaf called *gongura* or *ambada* is an important ingredient of most soups (*rasam, dal* or *sambar*) and is also ground with red or green chillies into a fiery chutney. You will also find mutton or chicken dishes blended with a gravy or dry curry base of green leafy vegetables like spinach (*palak*), gongura or fenugreek (*methi*). Dry-fried fish or pepper-coated chicken is commonly served as a starter. Curried prawns are popular in coastal Andhra. Hyderabad is well known for its *biryani*, steam-baked saffron-flavoured rice layered over meat, *haleem* (ground meat), paya soup and paratha breads.

In Tamil Nadu, many eateries serve set vegetarian meals which are generally simple and mildly spiced. The meal usually comprises a variety of vegetables, *sambar*, rice, *rasam*, papadums, sweets and sometimes chappatis. Chettinad restaurants, also gaining popularity across Tamil Nadu, serve a variety of meat dishes in spicy gravies that are strong on pepper, chilli, garlic and ginger. Seafood lovers will be in their element in coastal Kerala, where accessibility and tourist awareness combine to ensure that delicious and affordable fish dishes abound.

Meal or *thali*
A 'meal' or a *thali* refers to a simple set menu with a fixed price served to everyone. It is usually good, quick, reasonably priced and freshly prepared. A vegetarian meal usually includes vegetables, chappatis, pulses, rice, pickles, yoghurts and sauces, and occasionally a local sweet. A *thali* is served on a metal platter, with the individual items in separate little bowls. Non-vegetarian meals usually include mutton, chicken or fish dishes.

Ice cream
Well-known brands are Vadilal and Amul, plus international names such as Walls and Baskin-Robbins. Amul also offers Indian ice cream called *kulfis*. Avoid ice cream from hawkers.

Fruits
Papaya, pineapples, guava, jackfruit, oranges, mangoes, grapes and sweet limes are among the many fruits grown in Southern India, and other fruits such as apples and pears are also available. You can buy fruit and vegetables such as cucumbers from markets, street-side vendors and hawkers with pushcarts anywhere in India. Bargaining helps bring down the price. Peel the fruit before eating it, or at least wash it in purified water.

Food and drink

WHERE TO EAT
Restaurant price
guide

The following categories
are based on the price of
an average meal per
person, excluding drinks:

★ Less than Rs 200
★★ Rs 200–500
★★★ Rs 500–1,000
★★★★ above Rs 1,000

Bangalore
Mavalli Tiffin Room ★

A famed vegetarian fast-
food eatery with South
Indian staples. A more
leisurely lunch can be
enjoyed upstairs.
*Lalbagh Road. Tel: 0802
222 0022. Open: 6.30–
11am, 12.30–2.45pm,
3.30–7.30pm, 8–9.30pm.*

Palm Grove ★

Spice fiends and
vegetarians are well
catered for at this jolly
hotel restaurant.
*Ballal Residency, 74/4, III
Cross, Residency Road.
Tel: 0802 559 7277.
Open: 7am–10.30pm.*

Koshy's ★★

Bustling Koshy's is three
eateries in one. There's
fine dining in Jewel Box,
Parade Café for coffee or
a snack, and Chill-Out
for fancy ice cream.

*39 Saint Marks Road.
Tel: 0802 221 3793.
www.koshys.com.
Open: 9am–11.30pm.*

Chennai
Ceylon Restaurant ★

Decent Sri Lankan fare.
*15 Kennet Lane, Egmore.
Tel: 0442 819 3374.
Open: 8am–11pm.*

Saravana Bhavan ★

This friendly and fun
place serves up well-
presented cheap eats.
*101 Dr Radhakrishnan
Salai. Tel: 0442 811 5977.
Open: 7am–11pm. Other
branches at 293 Peter's
Road, 21 Kennet Lane,
209 NSC Bose Lane and
48 Anna Salai.*

Copper Chimney ★★

Meaty North Indian
tandooris are served here.
*Cathedral Road,
Teynampet. Tel: 0442 811
5770. Open: noon–3pm &
6–11.30pm.*

Annalakshmi ★★★

Sumptuously decorated,
this vegetarian concern
has branches scattered
around Asia.
*804 Anna Salai. Tel: 0442
852 5109. www.
annalakshmichennai.com.
Open: noon–3pm &
7–11pm.*

The Rain Tree ★★★

Authentic Chettinad
(south Tamil Nadu)
food. It can be spicy.
*Taj Connemara, 2 Binny
Road. Tel: 0446 600 0000.
Open: 7.30–11.45 pm.*

601 ★★★★

International and Indian
dishes are expertly
conjured up by chefs
before your eyes.
*The Park Hotel, 601 Anna
Salai. Tel: 0444 267 6000.
www.theparkhotels.com.
Open: 24 hours.*

Peshawari ★★★★

This grand hotel
restaurant does fab kebab
and top-notch *daal.*
*Chola Sheraton,
10 Cathedral Road,
Gopalapuram. Tel: 0442
811 0101. Open: noon–
3pm & 7.45–11.45pm.*

Hyderabad
Angeethi ★

A jolly place to eat Punjab
and *tandoori* cuisine.
*701–703 Reliance Classic
Building, Road No. 1,
Banjara Hills. Tel: 0406
525 5550. Open: 12.30–
3.30pm & 7–10.30pm.*

Bawarchi ★★

The seafood is good, and
there are tasty *biriyani*
options and curries too.

Plot No. 66, Main Road, RTC crossroads.
Tel: 0406 711 2871.
Open: 11.30am–11pm.

Southern Spice ★★
Mostly Andhra cuisine, the food is as piquant as the name suggests.
Road No. 2, Banjara Hills. Tel: 0402 335 3802. Open: 12.15–3.30pm & 7–11.30pm.

Fusion 9 ★★★
Trendy eatery, though prices are reasonable. The wine list – both international and Indian – is another draw.
6-3-249/A, Ist Avenue, Road No. 1, Banjara Hills. Tel: 0406 557 7722.
Open: noon–3.30pm & 7pm–midnight.

Touch of Class ★★★
Andhra Pradesh cuisine, with Chinese, Continental and other Indian dishes.
Central Court Hotel, 6-1-71 Lakdikapul.
Tel: 0402 323 2323.
www.thecentralcourt.com.
Open: noon–3pm & 7–11pm.

Deccan Pavilion ★★★★
Smart hotel café with a slew of cuisines whipped up in five show kitchens.
ITC Kakatiya, 63-3-1187, Begumpet. Tel: 0402 340

0132. www.starwoodhotels. com. Open: 24 hours.

Kochi
Kashi Art Café ★
Attached to an art gallery, Kashi serves coffee, cakes and snacks.
Burgher Street, Fort Cochin. Tel: 0484 221 5769. Open: 8.30am–7.30pm.

Chariot Beach ★★
Try the seafood, cooked on the outdoor grill.
Corner of Princess Street, Near Children's Park, Fort Cochin. Tel: 0484 221 7807/984 705 7745.
Open: 8am–11pm.

History ★★★
The menu draws on the gastronomic traditions of Kochi's numerous settlers and denizens.
Brunton Boatyard, Fort Cochin.
Tel: 0484 221 5461.
www.cghearth.com.
Open: 7.30–10.30 or 11pm.

Travancore ★★★★
Convivial surroundings, warm service and top-notch food are all assured at Travancore.
Trident Hotel, Bristow Road, Willingdon Island. Tel: 0484 308 1000.
www.tridenthotels.com.

Open: 6.30–10.30am, 12.30–3pm & 7–11pm.

Thiruvananthapuram
Daavat ★
Cheap and cheerful, this hotel restaurant near the station serves the normal range of Indian and international food.
Hotel Regency, Manjalikulam Cross Road, Thampanoor.
Tel: 0471 233 0377.
Open: daily 7am–11pm.

Casa Bianca ★★
This friendly Swedish-run pizzeria and bread shop is ideal when spice fatigue is setting in, though there are some Indian options too.
96 MP Appan Road, Vazhuthacaud, opposite Heera Park.
Tel: 0471 233 8323. www. casabiancatrivandrum. com. Open: Tue–Sun noon–10pm.

Coffee Beanz ★★
A branch of a popular local chain with a range of international coffees and snacks.
Near Women's College, Vazhuthacaud.
Tel: 0471 232 3301. Open: Mon–Sat 11am–10pm, Sun 9am–10pm.

Land of spice: coastal cuisine

Keralan cooking uses coconut milk, coconut flesh or coconut oil in most dishes. There are regional variations and differences between the preparations of the Moplah community of Malabari Muslims, the Syrian Christians and the other Malayalis. Arabian influences are obvious in the Moplah cuisine, where dried fruits and nuts are used for gravies and *biryani*. English influences are apparent in the dishes of Syrian Christians.

Breakfast may include *puttu*, a steamed rice cake that is sometimes served with bananas or fish. *Idiappams* are steamed rice noodles topped with ground coconut and often served with curried vegetables or meats. *Appam* is a flat, chappati-like rice cake with crispy edges, and is a popular breakfast item.

A chef at the Park Hotel, Chennai

Typical vegetarian dishes, common to all communities, are *avail*, mixed vegetables in a grated coconut sauce with or without fruits and nuts, *thoren*, vegetables fried or steamed with coconut, mustard and occasionally also green papaya, and *olen*, a coconut-based bean and gourd curry. These are served as accompaniments to rice, with *sambar*, a lentil soup with vegetables, and *rasam*, a flavoured broth. *Pachkkary shtew* is a typical tangy vegetable stew, very popular in central Kerala, especially among the Syrian Christians. It is usually eaten with *appam*.

Other vegetarian favourites are *cheera* curry, which is spinach curried with coconut milk, and *vendekka varathathu*, which is roasted okra. Vegetarian Keralan meals, influenced by Ayurvedic principles, are popular at Ayurvedic resorts.

As is to be expected from a state with 44 rivers, backwaters, innumerable lakes and a long coastline, fish and seafood is a mainstay of the cuisine of Kerala. Sardines, kingfish, squid, tiger prawns and crabs are the usual catches along the coast, while *karimeen*, or pearl-spot, is the classic catch of the backwaters. The lakes also yield sizeable fish catches. Fish is usually prepared in coconut curry (*meen pahichadhu*), in chilli-hot curry (*meen vevichatu*), with sour fruit and chillies (*meen kodampuli*), in thick curries (*meen mappas*), in grated coconut and spices curry (*meen peera*), in a mango curry (*mathi curry*), in a banana leaf (*meen pollichathu*) or pickled. Other popular fish dishes are *meen moily* in a mildly spiced coconut curry or *meen varathathu*, fried fish. Curried prawns are also very popular.

Chicken curry is very popular and there are many versions such as *kozhy thenga varutharachathu* (curried with fried ground coconut) or *kozhy varathathu* (fried chicken) at restaurants in Kerala. Ducks are often reared by the people living along the backwaters. You can get *thengapal chertha tharavu*, which is curried duck in coconut milk, or *varutha tharavukari*, which is duck roasted with dry red chillies, accompanied with tapioca or *appam*.

Mutton (goat) is eaten more often than lamb in India. *Attirachi mappas* is a typical mutton curry of Kerala. Mutton *biryani*, steam-baked rice layered on mutton and boiled eggs, is extremely popular in northern Kerala.

Among the four states of Southern India, you are most likely to find beef on restaurant menus in Kerala because of the sizeable Muslim and Christian populations. *Mattirachi*

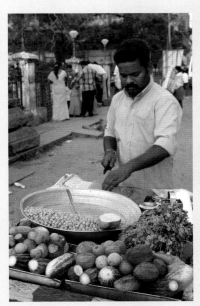
Street-food stall, Thiruvananthapuram

peralan is beef in a hot and spicy curry. Some Malayali Hindus also eat buffalo beef.

Pork is eaten by the Hindus and Christians of Kerala.

The various types of bread include *Kerala parathas*, fried wheat flour, pancakes such as *appam*, which is made from rice with a spongy centre, or the crisp *pathiri*. *Puttu* is a popular breakfast made from rice-flour dough. Rice noodles are called *idi-appam*.

Towards the end of the meal, the people of Kerala eat yoghurt-based dishes such as coconut-flavoured curd called *pachadi*. *Payasam* is a popular pudding made from sugared rice or vermicelli.

Accommodation

Southern India has a huge variety of accommodation, ranging from family-run guesthouses to upmarket resorts. Visitors can expect to find a hotel that suits their needs and their budget in most towns. However, hotels in India suffer from a number of problems that visitors may not have experienced elsewhere, such as dust, mosquitoes and other insects, power cuts and water shortages.

Price categories

Hotels are graded from one-star to five-star deluxe, with categories of four-star and above given by the central government authorities and the lower star classifications by the state government. Hotels are judged on a number of pre-determined standards, from ambience and room size to the qualifications of the staff, services and facilities.

Five-star deluxe hotels have extensive facilities, including modern rooms, round-the-clock room service, swimming pool, bar, 24-hour coffee shop, and restaurant. Five-star and four-star hotels are a cut below the five-star deluxe hotels, while three-star hotels maintain reasonably good standards without the frills of a five-star deluxe.

Budget stays

India has many modestly priced hotels. Most of them are located near railway stations, bus stations or near the market, and standards vary considerably. Some can be great value for money, while others are downright dirty.

Before booking into a really low-priced hotel, it is important to inspect the rooms to check the standards of cleanliness and to see that everything works.

Forest lodges

The forest department has lodges and resthouses inside most Indian wildlife reserves. Like the other government guesthouses, these too are beautifully located but are rarely well managed and can be difficult to book prior to arrival.

Privately owned lodges, resorts and camps are generally located near the entrance to or in peripheral areas of the reserves. These are organised for visitors to the wildlife reserves.

Government guesthouses

Government guesthouses, such as the Circuit Houses in cities, and the Public Works Department Resthouses, which are located outside the cities and towns, are often grand colonial buildings with equally impressive rooms. Most of them have highly desirable locations, but unfortunately many of them are poorly managed and maintained. Moreover, rooms are generally reserved for government officials, so finding accommodation can be difficult.

Heritage hotels

Buildings built before 1935 that have been opened for visitors are called heritage hotels in India. This is not a homogeneous concept, and it covers a variety of types of accommodation, from five-star deluxe palace hotels to bungalows run by the owners.

In Kerala, heritage hotels, such as Ayisha Manzil at Thalasseri and Harivihar at Kozhikode, are still partially occupied by their owners. Other old residences, including River Retreat at Cheruthuruthy and Malaabar House Residency, have been converted into hotels. A unique concept in Kerala is the relocation of old wooden houses to new sites, such as beaches and backwaters, to create 'heritage resorts'. Surya Samudra, Somatheeram and Nikki's Nest at Chowara south of Kovalam, and Coconut Lagoon at Kumarakom, are almost entirely comprised of transplanted old wooden buildings. Palaces in Mysore have been converted into hotels offering luxury facilities.

Plantation houses

It is possible to stay at working plantations, in Munnar, Kodagu district, Kumily near Thekkadi (at the entrance to the Periyar Tiger Reserve), and on the way from Thekkadi to Munnar. These plantations all have

Lalitha Mahal Palace Hotel, Mysore

converted heritage houses, as well as newly built resorts.

Railway retiring rooms
Most railway stations have private rooms and dormitories that are handy for travellers. These are in high demand and are almost always full.

Tourist bungalows
The government-supported tourism corporations of Kerala, Karnataka, Tamil Nadu and Andhra own and manage tourist bungalows in their respective states. These can be good-value options for travellers, but standards vary considerably. At some destinations, they could be the only places to stay.
Andhra Pradesh Tourism Development Corporation *www.tourisminap.com*
Karnataka State Tourism Development Corporation
www.karnatakaholidays.net
Kerala Tourism Development Corporation *www.ktdc.com*
Tamil Nadu Tourism Development Corporation *www.tamilnadutourism.org*
Pondicherry Tourism
http://tourism.pondicherry.gov.in

Upmarket resorts
Resorts at the beaches or hill stations have a special attraction because of their location. They provide idyllic settings and a vast range of facilities. Some of the popular resorts are at the beaches of Kovalam and Marari, the backwaters around Kumarakom, the

hill town of Munnar in Kerala, the hill stations of Ooty and Kodaikanal, and the beaches near Mahabalipuram in Tamil Nadu. Such resorts are heavily booked in the winter months from October to March, so early advance reservations are recommended.

Accommodation price guide
Prices are based on a double room per night for two people, with breakfast, in high season. Some of the more upmarket hotels offer package deals through international travel agents, which can reduce the daily rate considerably.

- ★ under Rs 1,000
- ★★ Rs 1,000–3,000
- ★★★ Rs 3,000–6,000
- ★★★★ over Rs 6,000

Bangalore
Hotels in Bangalore can be on the costly side, and renting a short-stay apartment is sometimes a better option.

Hotel Empire International ★★
Centrally located establishment providing cheerfully decorated accommodation with non-stop hot water, internet access and an in-house restaurant. The travel desk can help with your onward arrangements. The same group also offers service apartments.
36 Church Street. Tel: 0802 559 3743. www.hotelempireinternational.com

Email: *hotelempireintl@ hotmail.com*

Tricolour Hotel ★★

Its proximity to the bus and train stations makes Tricolour a convenient base for a short stay. Rooms, which come in various categories, are well equipped and easy on the eye.

Tank Bund Road, Majestic.
Tel: 0804 127 9090.
www.ibchotels-resorts.com. Email: tricolour@ibchotels.co.in

Chennai

As is the case in many Indian state capitals, Chennai's hotels can be pricey and quickly fill up.

Hotel Chandra Park ★

Tasteful, air-conditioned rooms, a decent buffet breakfast and reasonable prices make Hotel Chandra Park a popular option. Its location, opposite Egmore Station, is another boon.

9 Gandhi Irwin Road, Egmore.
Tel: 0442 819 1177.
www. hotelchandrapark.com.

Email: *info@ hotelchandrapark.com*

The Park ★★★★

This impossibly stylish design hotel inhabits the location of a former film studio, and draws on the artistic theme in its dazzling décor. Sleek and chic, the service, comfort and facilities are equal to the aesthetics. If your pockets are deep enough, it's well worth shelling out.

601 Anna Salai.
Tel: 0444 267 6000.
www.theparkhotels.com.
Email: resv.che@ theparkhotels.com

Treehouse accommodation in the hills of Kerala

Hyderabad
Hotel Suhail ★
It cannot be described as swanky, but this budget option has welcoming service, peaceful and good-sized rooms and 24-hour hot water. Be warned that the approach is not lit at night.
4-1-527, Troop Bazar, Behind GPO Abids.
Tel: 0402 461 0299.
www.hotelsuhail.in.
Email: info@hotelsuhail.in

Athidhi Guest House ★★
Simple three-bedroom service apartments in a peaceful residential area, with retail and dining options close at hand. Breakfast is included, while lunch and dinner can be rustled up upon request.
Valley View Apartments, Road No. 13A, Happy Valley, Off Road No. 13, Banjara Hills.
Tel: 0402 331 2649.
athidhiguesthouse.com.
Email: padma. athidhi@gmail.com

Kerala Backwaters
Oberoi Vrinda ★★★★
Kerala's extraordinary backwaters cannot be seen in more comfort and style than on the *Vrinda* motor vessel. With conditions akin to a top-class hotel, exemplary service and a fabulous menu, the package is rounded off with a well-thought-out programme of entertainment and excursions.
Departs from Vembanad Lake.
Tel: 0484 266 9595.
www.oberoihotels.com.
Email: sharad.datta@ tridenthotels.com

Kochi
Though Ernakulam has a range of cheaper accommodation options, for a more atmospheric stay visitors should head for the Fort Cochin side of the water. Some upmarket places can be found on Willingdon Island.

Ramada Resort ★★★
Combining a relaxed, resort-style ambience with easy access to the city, the Ramada offers the best of both worlds. Accommodation here takes the form of über-stylish rooms on stilts, set around a pool, and lush gardens. There is a fitness centre, spa and Ayurvedic centre.
Kumbalam South.
Tel: 0484 301 1100.
www.ramadacochin.com
Email: reservations@ ramadacochin.com

Brunton Boatyard ★★★★
Part of a series of unique heritage hotels that draw upon their locations' history and environment, Brunton Boatyard boasts elegant, period-style rooms, fine dining and a top spot in the heart of Fort Cochin. Alternative group properties can also be found in other parts of Kochi, at Periyar Reserve, on Bangaram Island and elsewhere in and around Kerala.
1/498 Fort Cochin.
Tel: 0484 301 1711.
www.cghearth.com.
Email: kg.cghearthhotels.com

Trident ★★★★
Smart and tasteful, the Trident has sumptuous, comfortable rooms surrounding a large pool in a courtyard. The excellent Ayurveda centre

...and superior eateries are further reason to stay here, at a slight remove from the city's main action, on Willingdon Island.
Bristow Road, Willingdon Island.
Tel: 0484 308 1000.
www.tridenthotels.com.
Email: reservations@ tridenthotels.com

Thiruvananthapuram

Hotel Regency ★
Welcoming staff, a peaceful location and two restaurants recommend this good-value and conveniently located option. Rooms are en-suite with satellite TV and some are air conditioned.
Manjalikulam Cross Road, Thampanoor.
Tel: 0471 233 0377.
www.hotelregency.com.
Email:
info@hotelregency.com

A villa at the Ramada Resort, Kochi

Practical guide

Arriving
International
Anna International Airport in Chennai is the main gateway to Southern India. Bangalore and Hyderabad are also served by international flights. The airports of Kerala mainly receive international flights from Middle-Eastern countries.

Air France *www.airfrance.com*
Air India *www.airindia.com*
American Airlines *www.aa.com*
British Airways
www.britishairways.com
Cathay Pacific Airways
www.cathaypacific.com
Continental Airlines
www.continental.com
Delta Airlines *www.delta.com*
Japan Airlines *www.jal.com*
Lufthansa *www.lufthansa.com*

Overloaded bus, Karnataka

Malaysia Airlines
www.malaysiaairlines.com
Qantas Airways *www.qantas.com*

Domestic
Domestic airlines, such as Indian Airlines, Jet Airways and Sahara, connect the gateway cities of Mumbai and Chennai with Southern Indian destinations.

Air Deccan *www.deccanairlines.in*
Air India and **Indian Airlines**
www.airindia.com
GoAir *www.goair.in*
IndiGo *www.goindigo.in*
Jet Airways *www.jetairways.com*
Kingfisher Airlines
www.flykingfisher.com
Paramount Airways
www.paramountairways.com
Sahara Airlines
www.saharaairlines.co.in
Spicejet *www.spicejet.com*

Airports and customs
At the time of writing, visitors are allowed to bring into the country personal items, alcoholic drinks up to a maximum of 1 litre, 50 cigars or 200 cigarettes or 250g of tobacco, and duty-free gifts up to a maximum value of Rs 5,000.

Any expensive personal effects or equipment such as binoculars and cameras should be registered for re-export. Keep registration numbers handy, especially for laptops, cameras

The hills of the Western Ghats

and other expensive equipment, as these are required when you fill in the re-export form. There is a departure tax for international flights, but most airlines add it to their fare.

Airline offices

Air France *City ticket office, Level 1, 42 Kubers, Pantheon Road, Chennai–600008. Tel: 180 011 0055. www.airfrance.in*

Air India *19 Rukmini Laxmipathy Road, Egmore, Chennai–600008. Tel: 0442 855 4477. www.airindia.com*

American Airlines *Prince Centre, 248 Anna Salai, Thousand Lights, Chennai–600006. Tel: 0442 859 2915. www.americanairlines.in*

British Airways *Sigma Wing, 177 Anna Salai. Chennai–600002. Tel: 984 037 7470. www.britishairways.com*

Cathay Pacific Airways *Spencer's Travel Services Ltd, 2nd floor, Heavitree 47, Spur Tank Road, Chetpet, Chennai–600031. Tel: 0444 298 8400. www.cathaypacific.in*

Continental Airlines *Stic Travels Pvt. Ltd, 672 Temple Tower, Anna Salai, Nandanam, Chennai–600035. Tel: 0442 433 0211. www.continental.com*

Delta Airlines *Ground floor, 144/145 Malavika Centre, Kodambakkam High Road, Nungambakkam, Chennai–600034. Tel: 0442 824 0073. www.delta.com*

Japan Airlines *Hotel Ambassador Pallava, 53 (old No.) or 30 (new No.) Monteith Road, Egmore, Chennai–600008. Tel: 0442 859 2333. www.in.jal.com*

Lufthansa *167 Anna Salai, Nandanam, Chennai–600002. Tel: 0442 256 9393. www.lufthansa-india.com*

Malaysia Airlines *Arihant Nico Park,
90 Dr Radhakrishnan Salai, Mylapore,
Chennai–600004. Tel: 0442 256 0084.
www.malaysiaairlines.com*
Qantas Airways *72–75 Dr
Radhakrishnan Salai, Mylapore,
Chennai–600004. Tel: 0442 811 3870.
www.qantas.com*

Climate

Southern India has a tropical climate,
with temperatures ranging from 18°C
(64°F) to 35°C (95°F).

Seasons

April to June (summer) is the hottest
period and November to February
(winter) is the coolest. The coast can
become humid in the warm months.
The interior hills of Munnar and
Periyar Tiger Reserve are more pleasant
than the coast in summer, but they can
be chilly in winter.

The monsoon

The southwest monsoon blows in from
the Arabian Sea and is condensed by
the cooler climes of the Western Ghats,
causing torrential rains, lashing waves
and powerful winds in early June.
There is another wet spell in November
and December, which is caused by the
retreating monsoon from the eastern
Bay of Bengal.

Clothing

Loose-fitting light cottons are most
suited to the warm and humid weather
of Kerala, but it is a good idea to carry

**WEATHER CONVERSION
CHART**

25.4mm = 1 inch
°F = 1.8 × °C + 32

a jacket or a sweater for the evenings,
especially if destinations in the Western
Ghats, such as Wayanad, Munnar and
Periyar, are part of your itinerary. Long-
sleeved clothes in light colours provide
some protection from mosquitoes.

   Wear comfortable shoes and sandals
that allow your feet to breathe. Laundry
is inexpensive and rarely takes more
than 24 hours, but delicate clothes
should be washed personally.

Electricity

Electric current is 230–240 AC, 50
cycles. Electric power cuts are frequent
but usually short-lived. Bring a surge
protector to protect any electrical
equipment from power fluctuations.
Most hotel rooms have both two-pin
and three-pin sockets.

he climate in Kerala is ideal for growing tea

Getting around

Boats

Boats provide a good way of seeing the landscape along the backwaters. You can take a tourist cruise or charter a whole boat.

Buses

Buses are an economical and convenient way to reach places off the railway network in Kerala, but they are rarely the most comfortable means of transport. The Kerala State Road Transport Corporation (KSRTC) has buses connecting the cities, towns and most of the important villages, but you may have to change if visiting remote places or travelling very long distances. Signs at bus stands and on the buses themselves are sometimes in Malayalam, but you are likely to find English-speaking passengers willing to help and interpret. Bus stations at the cities and at most of the bigger bus stands have information counters. Some buses have a section of seats reserved for women.

Private buses are usually more comfortable. Some operators run air-conditioned coaches, express buses and overnight 'sleeper' coaches (with bunks), but you must be prepared for loud music. Better quality air-conditioned European coaches now operate between cities. Bookings are computerised in many cities, and it is possible to reserve seats in advance.

Local buses run in cities such as Thiruvananthapuram, Kochi and Kozhikode, as well as the large towns. They are a cheap means of transport, though by no means the quickest or most comfortable option.

Cars and motorbikes

Hiring a car with a driver provides opportunities to travel off the beaten track and see the beautiful scenery of Kerala. Most drivers speak English and

Southern India gets hit annually by the monsoon

us station at Idukki

he local language, and can act as nterpreters to ask directions or interact vith locals. The rates are calculated on he basis of hours or days, with a roportionate kilometre allowance. If ou hire a car for more than a day, the night halt charge' includes the driver's xpenses. The driver will also expect a ip at the end of the tour.

Motorbikes are usually available to ire at tourist destinations. An lternative is the scooter, which has a ockable place for small items and a pare tyre on the back. Mopeds enerally have no gears and are suitable nly for travelling short distances.

You should always check the terms nd conditions before hiring (third party nsurance is compulsory in India). An nternational driving licence is advisable.

Bring a helmet with you or buy one in Kerala. Most travellers hiring motorbikes usually bring their own gloves, leathers, boots and other protective clothing. However you travel, be prepared to face some truly horrendous roads and driving.

Cycling
Bicycles are really only good for local travel in cities and towns, unless you are a real enthusiast who wants to make long-distance journeys along the coast or attempt challenging rides in the hills. Bicycles can be hired in most cities, towns and villages; they are heavy and do not have gears, but they are good for seeing some of the quieter areas of town, or for travelling on narrow streets. Some operators now offer

imported mountain bikes for hire in popular tourist centres.

On the roadsides you will find repair shops that are reasonably priced. Before you set off, check the tyres and the general condition of the bicycle, and that the bell and lights work. It may be a good idea to bring lights with you, plus a cord to strap down your luggage, as these are not easily available in India. Those travelling with children may find it useful to bring a basket along or get one made. Do not leave your rucksack or any other luggage on the bicycle, as it could be an invitation to thieves. If you bring your own bicycle with you, carry plenty of spares and a repair kit.

Ferries
Public ferries can be a convenient and economical means of seeing the backwaters. Ferries from Ernakulam, Fort Kochi and Willingdon Island in Kochi carry small vehicles such as motorbikes.

Taxis and rickshaws
Taxis are available at airports, railway stations and at taxi stands in the cities.

A boat on the backwaters brimming with happy daytrippers

Make sure you negotiate the rate for the trip before setting off.

Auto-rickshaws are noisy and uncomfortable three-wheel vehicles, with a driver in front and a bench or seats for two or three passengers at the back. They are more economical than taxis and convenient for negotiating the crowded and narrow streets because of their smaller size.

Trains
Trains are a reliable and usually punctual method of travel in Southern India. Overnight train travel saves both hotel expenses and time, and Indrail passes are convenient if you are planning to spend a lot of time on the rail network in India (though expensive for local travel within Kerala).

Train travel is popular and advance reservation is essential. The ticketing is computerised and there is a tourist window for those paying foreign currency at some stations, which can save the trouble of standing in queues. A few trains, such as the Rajdhani Express, have air-conditioned first-class carriages with coupés or four-bedded cabins. Two-tier and three-tier air-conditioned sleeper cars have curtains along the aisles, and the folding bunks have reading lights and bedding provided. Second class is overcrowded and uncomfortable, with narrow, hard couches. Some trains have air-conditioned cars with seats. There are tables that fold down from the chair

back in front, magazine racks and overhead luggage racks.

Vendors sell bottled water, soft drinks and snacks on board and at stations, and simple meals are served on most trains, but it's a good idea to carry an adequate supply of food and water.

For up-to-date details of train services, consult the bi-monthly publication the *Thomas Cook Overseas Timetable*, available to buy online at *www.thomascookpublishing.com* or by telephoning *01733 416477*.

Health
Most visitors are immunised against polio, typhoid, tetanus and Hepatitis A and B before a visit to India. For longer trips, Japanese B encephalitis, meningitis, TB and rabies vaccinations may be appropriate.

Take dietary precautions to prevent diarrhoea and intestinal upsets, and make sure that you slap on the sun block, as many travellers suffer sunburn and heatstroke from spending time on the beaches without adequate protection. If you get bitten by a dog, monkey or other animal, an anti-rabies shot is essential. Ticks and leeches are common in the Western Ghats, and tick bites can cause typhus.

Hospitals and medical facilities
Generally, Southern India has good doctors and there are clinics and hospitals in the cities and in most large towns.

Malaria

Malaria is a serious problem, so see your doctor before leaving home. If you have any symptoms, consult a doctor. Also, protect yourself against mosquito bites by covering yourself completely at night and using repellents.

Pharmacies

There are medical stores in cities, large towns and most villages. You will also find medical stores on the highways. The stores usually have local equivalents of most medicines, but carry an emergency supply of essential and prescribed medicines.

Internet

India is a computer-oriented society and there are plenty of places to get online throughout Kerala, though options may be more limited in smaller towns.

Media

You will have access to Mumbai or Bangalore editions of national English language dailies, such as the *Times of India* and *Indian Express,* as well as locally published English dailies. News magazines such as *India Today*, *The Week* and *Outlook* are also available at newsstands and bookstores.

Almost all hotels have satellite TV in their rooms, with a choice of channels for Indian and international programmes. Besides the foreign channels, you can also access Indian news in English.

Money

The Indian currency is the rupee, which is divided into units of 100 *paise*. Notes are printed in denominations of Rs 1,000, 500, 100, 50, 20, 10 and 5, while coins are minted in Rs 10, 5, 2, 1, 0.50, 0.25, 0.10 and 0.05. Indians write Rs 100,000 as Rs 1,00,000 (one *lakh*), with 100 *lakhs* making a *crore*.

Currency exchange

It is not possible to order rupees in your home country, so you will need to

A Shiva shrine

The sun rises over a houseboat on Kerala's backwaters

hange currency on arrival at the
irport. Money exchange is not really a
roblem in India as banks, hotels and
icensed private moneychangers or
uthorised dealers will happily change
ollars, euros or sterling for rupees.
Collect your encashment certificate,
which will help you when you need
o reconvert currency. The certificates
lso help you to pay in rupees at tourist
quota counters at railway stations.

Traveller's cheques
Thomas Cook's traveller's cheques
re widely accepted for exchange
and as payment at hotels, and they
are a relatively safe way of carrying
money.

Credit cards
Almost all star-category hotels and
resorts, expensive restaurants and
established shops accept VISA and
MasterCard.

Tipping
It is customary to tip 10 per cent at
restaurants, Rs 10 to Rs 20 each to
hotel porters, and Rs 50 to Rs 100 a day
to drivers.

Internet cafés, Kochi

Passports and visas

A visa is essential for all visitors to India except those from Nepal and Bhutan. It is valid for six months from date of issue and can be obtained from the Indian embassy in most countries. You should also carry a set of photocopies in case you lose the originals.

Indian embassies abroad

Australia
3–5 Moonah Place, Yarralumla, Canberra. Tel: (2) 6273 3999. www.hcindia-au.org

Canada
10 Springfield Road, Ottawa, KIM IC9. Tel: (613) 744 3751. www.hciottawa.ca

New Zealand
10th floor, Princess Tower,
180 Molesworth St, Wellington.
Tel: (04) 473 6390. www.hicomind.org.nz

South Africa
852 Schoeman Street, Arcadia 0083,
Pretoria. Tel: (012) 3425 392.
www.indiainsouthafrica.com

UK
India House, Aldwych, London
WC2B 4NA. Tel: (020) 7836 8484.
www.hcilondon.in

USA
2107 Massachusetts Avenue, NW,
Washington DC 20008. Tel: (202) 939
8888. www.indianembassy.org

Photography

See p23.

Post and freight

Postal services in India range from excellent to very unreliable. Send letters, postcards and parcels only from the big cities and towns and make sure the covers are franked in your presence at the counter. Important mail should be sent by registered post with a registration receipt and an attached acknowledgement card to be returned signed. Airmail and speed-post services are available at most large post offices. Stamps can be bought at the counters. Poste restante facilities, which most travellers find reliable, are available at most post offices. Leading courier services like DHL have offices in important destinations like Kozhikode, Kochi and Thiruvananthapuram, which a local courier service, called *angadia*, operates to smaller towns and villages. It is possible to send air-freight from airports like Kozhikode, Kochi and Thiruvananthapuram. The railways and some bus services also take domestic cargo.

Safety and security

Southern India is a fairly safe place to travel, although Goa's reputation as a drugs market does attract undesirable elements to the region, and there have been some high-profile incidents involving tourists. Remain alert and avoid out-of-the-way places at night. The vast majority of Indians who approach you during your travels will do so out of nothing more than friendliness and curiosity; however, bear in mind that being in a foreign environment can make tourists vulnerable.

India does suffer occasional terrorist incidents, though since the high-profile attacks in Mumbai in 2008, security at vulnerable sites has been stepped up considerably. While, in general, the different religions rub along quite well, tensions can flare up. Foreigners should avoid demonstrations and other likely sources of conflict.

Theft

Petty thefts are not uncommon in India. A money belt is a good way to carry handy cash, and an interior pocket is good for small valuables, spare cash and photocopies of documents.

Unattended baggage is an invitation for theft; keep a padlock and chain with you to secure your baggage to any immovable object if you need to leave it for any reason.

On trains, there are wires below the bunks to which you can secure your baggage with a chain and padlock.

Sustainable tourism

Thomas Cook is a strong advocate of ethical and fairly traded tourism and believes that the travel experience should be as good for the places visited as it is for the people who visit them. That's why we firmly support The Travel Foundation, a charity that develops solutions to help improve and protect holiday destinations, their environment, traditions and culture. To find out what you can do to make a positive difference to the places you travel to and the people who live there, please visit *www.thetravelfoundation.org.uk*

Telephones

India has well-developed telecommunications. Your mobile phone should pick up a signal in most places. There are call booths, called STD-ISD PCOs (public call offices) on all the important highways and in towns, cities and villages that are

Ranked autorickshaws, Andhra Pradesh

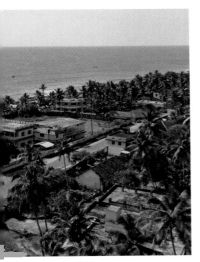

A fishing village amid palm groves near Varkala

usually cheaper than calling from hotels for national and international calls. Many PCOs have fax machines. Fax sending charges are based on phone rates with a supplement per page and the PCOs will receive facsimiles on your behalf for a per page fee. There are also coin-operated phones that are an inexpensive option for calling locally. Phonecards for mobile/cell phones called 'mobile cards' are available in India.

Time
Indian Standard Time is 5¹/₂ hours ahead of GMT.

Toilets
Public toilets are rarely clean in India, and they are almost always of the 'hole in the ground' variety. When travelling, look for hotels and smart restaurants that are likely to have westernised cloakrooms. Keep soap and a stock of tissues handy, and, especially if travelling with children, carry a supply of antiseptic wet wipes.

Travellers with disabilities
Unfortunately, India has limited facilities for disabled visitors. Getting around in a wheelchair on Indian pavements is difficult, few hotels and monuments have ramps for wheelchair access, and bathrooms are rarely accessible for the physically challenged. Hiring a car for the tour is a possible solution as Indian drivers are usually extremely helpful.

Weights and measures
India uses the metric system, where distances are in kilometres and weights in grams and kilograms. However, some imperial methods of measurement are still used in places.

CONVERSION TABLE

FROM	TO	MULTIPLY BY
Inches	Centimetres	2.54
Feet	Metres	0.3048
Yards	Metres	0.9144
Miles	Kilometres	1.6090
Acres	Hectares	0.4047
Gallons	Litres	4.5460
Ounces	Grams	28.35
Pounds	Grams	453.6
Pounds	Kilograms	0.4536
Tons	Tonnes	1.0160

To convert back, for example from centimetres to inches, divide by the number in the third column.

Index

Acknowledgements

Thomas Cook Publishing wishes to thank DAVID HENLEY/CPA MEDIA, to whom the copyright belongs, for the photographs in this book (except for the following images):
CHAWEEWAN CHUCHUAY 40, 61, 69, 70, 179
FLICKR/Adam Jones 15, Emmanuel Dyan 189
DREAMSTIME Jeremy Rich 83, Shailesh Nanal 95, Snehitdesign 119
INCREDIBLE INDIA 127
RAINER KRACK/CPA MEDIA 5, 33, 38, 41, 43, 47, 49, 71, 74, 173, 181, 182
PICTURES COLOUR LIBRARY/Monica Wells 26, Chris Caldicott 101
DINESH SHUKLA 79, 80, 129, 141
VASILE SZAKACS 1, 13, 23, 34, 37, 55, 63, 65, 66, 73, 75, 77, 81, 103, 121, 125, 139, 149, 153, 155, 157, 161, 163, 164, 168, 169, 175, 186, 188
THOMAS COOK TOUR OPERATIONS LTD 51, 58
WIKIMEDIA COMMONS/Haros 31, Rajesh Kakkanatt 56
WORLD PICTURES/PHOTOSHOT 113, 185

For CAMBRIDGE PUBLISHING MANAGEMENT LTD:
Project editor: Rosalind Munro
Typesetter: Trevor Double
Proofreader: Nick Newton
Indexer: Marie Lorimer

SEND YOUR THOUGHTS TO
BOOKS@THOMASCOOK.COM

We're committed to providing the very best up-to-date information in our travel guides and constantly strive to make them as useful as they can be. You can help us to improve future editions by letting us have your feedback. If you've made a wonderful discovery on your travels that we don't already feature, if you'd like to inform us about recent changes to anything that we do include, or if you simply want to let us know your thoughts about this guidebook and how we can make it even better – we'd love to hear from you.

Send us ideas, discoveries and recommendations today and then look out for your valuable input in the next edition of this title.

Emails to the above address, or letters to the traveller guides Series Editor, Thomas Cook Publishing, PO Box 227, Coningsby Road, Peterborough PE3 8SB, UK.

Please don't forget to let us know which title your feedback refers to!